The
Heidegger-Buber
Controversy

**Recent Titles in
Contributions in Philosophy**

Stalking Nietzsche
Raymond Angelo Belliotti

The Transient and the Absolute: An Interpretation of the Human Condition
and of Human Endeavor
Mordecai Roshwald

The Adventure of Philosophy
Luis E. Navia

Intentionalist Interpretation: A Philosophical Explanation and Defense
William Irwin

Natural Law Ethics
Philip E. Devine

Anglo-American Idealism, 1865–1927
W. J. Mander, editor

Two Views of Virtue: Absolute Relativism and Relative Absolutism
F. F. Centore

Liberty: Its Meaning and Scope
Mordecai Roshwald

Buddhist Epistemology
S. R. Bhatt and Anu Mehrotra

Partial Reason: Critical and Constructive Transformations of Ethics
and Epistemology
Sally E. Talbot

Certainty as a Social Metaphor: The Social and Historical Production of
Certainty in China and the West
Min Lin

Antisthenes of Athens: Setting the World Aright
Luis E. Navia

The Heidegger-Buber Controversy

The Status of the I–Thou

HAIM GORDON

Contributions in Philosophy, Number 81

GREENWOOD PRESS
Westport, Connecticut • London

Library of Congress Cataloging-in-Publication Data

Gordon, Hayim.
   The Heidegger-Buber controversy : the status of the I–Thou / Haim Gordon.
      p.   cm.—(Contributions in philosophy, ISSN 0084–926X ; no. 81)
   Includes bibliographical references and index.
   ISBN 0–313–30917–5 (alk. paper)
      1. Heidegger, Martin, 1889–1976.   2. Buber, Martin, 1878–1965.   3. Ontology.
   4. Intersubjectivity.   I. Title.   II. Series.
   B3279.H49G59   2001
   193—dc21   00–052122

British Library Cataloguing in Publication Data is available.

Library of Congress Catalog Card Number: 00–052122
ISBN: 0–313–30917–5
ISSN: 0084–926X

First published in 2001

Greenwood Press, 88 Post Road West, Westport, CT 06881
An imprint of Greenwood Publishing Group, Inc.
www.greenwood.com

Printed in the United States of America

The paper used in this book complies with the
Permanent Paper Standard issued by the National
Information Standards Organization (Z39.48–1984).

10 9 8 7 6 5 4 3 2 1

Contents

Acknowledgments   vii

Introduction   ix

PART I: HEIDEGGER'S FUNDAMENTAL
ONTOLOGY OF DASEIN

Section A: Being and Time

  1   Dasein and the World   5

  2   Dasein's Being-in, Care, and Truth   23

  3   Dasein and Temporality   41

Section B: Heidegger's Rejection of the I–Thou

  4   Phenomenology and Dasein   63

  5   Heidegger's First Critique of the I–Thou   77

  6   The I–Thou in Heidegger's Study of Kant   91

  7   Metaphysics and Logic   99

PART II: BUBER'S I–THOU

Section A: I and Thou

  8   First Presentation of the I–Thou   115

  9   Living the I–Thou   125

Section B: Beyond I and Thou

10   The I–Thou and Dialogue   139

11   Buber's Critique of Heidegger   151

12   Conclusion and Some Implications   159

Selected Bibliography   163

Index   167

Acknowledgments

Many people have helped me in the process of writing this difficult book. I cannot mention them all. I want to thank Professor Jimmy Weinblat and Professor Nahum Finger, who gave me time off and financial support for the research needed to undertake the writing. Much thanks also to my wife, Rivca Gordon, who read the manuscript and provided important criticism, in addition to giving me loving personal support.

Lately, I have also been blessed with the task of advising a large group of talented, enthusiastic, and challenging graduate students who are writing their theses with my guidance. These students have repeatedly challenged me to think on many philosophical topics and issues, including the topics that are at the core of this book. In a roundabout way, they have helped me to formulate my thoughts on Heidegger and Buber.

I have decided, therefore, to dedicate this book to six of my graduate students: Batya Bahat, Mika Elior, Efrat Manshuri, Rina Shtelman, Shlomit Tamari, and Sigal Tsoref.

Introduction

Martin Buber's book, *Ich und Du* [*I and Thou*], was first published in 1923. In this short book, Buber presented a detailed and profound outline of the ontology of the I–It and the I–Thou; this ontology later became the basis of what has been called his dialogical philosophy. Martin Heidegger's lengthy ontological study, *Sein und Zeit* [*Being and Time*], was first published in 1927. In that book he presented and developed his fundamental analysis of Dasein, the human entity. This analysis was central to his fundamental ontology, which, Heidegger believed, helped to raise again, in an appropriate manner, after two and a half millennia of evasion, the question of the meaning of Being. The attempt to think of the fundamental ontology of the human entity, while discussing and responding to the question of the meaning of Being, engaged Heidegger throughout his life.

In that same year, 1927, in his summer semester lecture course at the University of Marburg, which was many years later published as *The Basic Problems of Phenomenology*, Heidegger firmly rejected the ontological basis of the I–Thou.[1] Among other reasons for this rejection, Heidegger stated: "If the I–Thou represents a distinctive existence relationship, this cannot be recognized existentially, hence philosophically, as long as it is not asked what existence in general means."[2] Heidegger reiterated, very briefly, his rejection of the I–Thou in his 1928 winter semester lectures at the University of Marburg, which were many years later published as *Phenomenological Interpretation of Kant's "Critique of Pure Reason."*[3] Still, the ontological status of the I–Thou continued to perturb him. He again rejected the I–Thou, presenting a more detailed argument, in his summer semester lectures of 1928, which were his last lectures at the University of Marburg. After that, Heidegger moved to the University of Freiburg. Fifty years later, the last series of Marburg lectures was published as *The Metaphysical Foundations of Logic*.[4]

Buber may not have known of Heidegger's immediate response to the I–Thou, since Heidegger's above-mentioned lectures were published as books more than four decades after he presented them. However, in 1938, in a series of lectures presented at the Hebrew University in Jerusalem, later published as the long essay "What Is Man?" in his book *Between Man and Man*, Buber firmly repudiated Heidegger's fundamental analysis of Dasein and forcefully rejected Heidegger's fundamental ontology. Buber held that Heidegger's thinking rejects the I–Thou and the realm of the interhuman, and, therefore, this thinking lacks an attitude central to human existence.[5] In his discussion, Buber reached the conclusion that "Heidegger's self is *a closed system*."[6]

Fourteen years later, in 1952, in his book *Eclipse of God*, Buber again attacked Heidegger's ontology. His attack was directed to writings that appeared after *Sein und Zeit*. Buber's second attack related to writings by Heidegger which were published up until the late 1940s, including Heidegger's discussion of Friedrich Holderlin's poetry.[7] The reason Buber gives for his later attack on Heidegger's thinking is that it totally ignores the status of the I–Thou in the human–divine relationship.

Thus, there is a problem here. Two major twentieth-century thinkers on ontology firmly reject each other's central ideas. The rejection emerges, especially, in relation to the status of the I–Thou; however, it points to a much deeper disagreement. Unfortunately, there has been no scholarly philosophical attempt to examine these rejections and carefully to study the difference between the ontological writings of Heidegger and Buber.

Put succinctly, no scholar has ventured to clearly articulate the essence of the controversy between Heidegger and Buber on the status of the I–Thou and to show why and where they disagree, what is the philosophical source of this disagreement, and where they may have erred in their conclusions. Even prominent scholars who dealt in some detail with the ontologies of Buber and Heidegger have ignored the problem. One probable reason for shying away from discussing this problem is that few Heidegger scholars are well versed in Buber's thought, and vice versa.

Consider, for instance, Otto Poggeler's study, *Martin Heidegger's Path of Thinking*, which is considered to be a valuable summary and clarification of Heidegger's path of thinking.[8] A glance at the book's index reveals that Martin Buber appears as an entry only once. That index entry refers the reader to a note, which mentions that in *Eclipse of God*, Buber severely criticized Heidegger's interpretation of the sayings and the role of the Hebrew prophets. Poggeler does not go further; he does not examine the ontological and historical thinking that underlies Buber's severe critique. If he had undertaken this examination, he might have discovered that Buber's understanding of the Bible and of the lives, the missions, and the message of the Hebrew prophets is linked to his dialogical thinking and to his statements concerning the ontological status of the I–Thou. For instance, Buber believed that the Hebrew prophets engaged in an ongoing dialogue with God, which probably included many I–Thou encounters.

Robert E. Wood's short study, *Martin Buber's Ontology: An Analysis of "I and Thou"*[9] can serve as a contrary example. Wood ignores the Heidegger–Buber controversy concerning the status of the I–Thou. He mentions Heidegger seven or eight times in the course of his book, frequently comparing some of his thoughts to those of Buber. Yet nowhere in his study does Wood mention, or even hint about, the basic disagreement between Heidegger and Buber over the status of the I–Thou. Despite his careful analysis of *I and Thou*, despite his acquaintance with Buber's many writings, and despite his reading of some of Heidegger's relevant studies, Wood never indicates that he comprehended the basic disagreement between these two thinkers on the status of the I–Thou.

One study which purports to address some differences between Heidegger and Buber is Lawrence Vogel's *The Fragile "We": Ethical Implications of Heidegger's "Being and Time."*[10] Vogel mentions both Heidegger and Buber. Nevertheless, the careful reader is very soon disillusioned. Consider the first sentence of Vogel's book: "In his 'Letter on Humanism' Martin Heidegger claims that the fundamental *ontology* he works out in *Being and Time* offers a 'fundamental *ethics*.' "[11] To substantiate this claim, Vogel directs the reader to a page in the "Letter on Humanism." But when you examine the page you find that Heidegger made no such statement. A search through the rest of Heidegger's "Letter on Humanism" reveals nothing even remotely similar to the first sentence of Vogel's book.

No, Lawrence Vogel is not misreading Heidegger's "Letter on Humanism." He is spreading false statements. Indeed, his entire book engages in such bizarre hoodwinking. In short, Lawrence Vogel ignobly jumbles together superficial readings of Heidegger together with false statements—thus creating an embarrassment to serious scholarship.

A good scholarly paper, which compares some of the thoughts of Heidegger and Buber, is Heinrich Ott's study "Hermeneutic and Personal Structure of Language."[12] However, Ott, who discusses a later period in each thinker's life and is concerned with language, does not address the question of the status of the I–Thou. Consequently, from a scholarly perspective, examining the status of the I–Thou is virgin territory.

* * *

Someone may ask: Are you sure that Martin Heidegger was acquainted with and relating to Buber's thinking when he criticized the ontological status of the I–Thou? After all, Heidegger did not mention Buber specifically when he criticized and rejected the I–Thou.

True, in the above-mentioned books, Heidegger does not mention Martin Buber when briefly discussing and firmly rejecting the I–Thou as central to the ontology of human existence. What is more, to the best of my knowledge, Heidegger never mentioned Martin Buber in any other writings. Could it be that already in 1927, Heidegger, who looked favorably upon the Nazis, and a few years later publicly blessed their ideology, did not want to mention a Jewish scholar?—Perhaps.

Yet it is well known, and pretty much confirmed by historical research, that it was Martin Buber who coined the term I–Thou and who first suggested its broad manifestations in ontology. For instance, Rivka Horwitz has shown that the Catholic theologian Ferdinand Ebener may have influenced Buber's belief that you can only relate to God as a Thou. But Horwitz's research discloses that Ebener did not use the term I–Thou as describing an event central to a worthy human existence. Nor did Ebener present an ontology in which the I–Thou is central to the development of worthy human relations, including relations to nature. Martin Buber did.[13]

Furthermore, Buber has noted that he was influenced by Ludwig Feuerbach's manifesto, *Principles of the Philosophy of the Future*, published in 1843.[14] In that manifesto, Feuerbach uses the terms I and Thou and holds that they are central to describing what he termed the essence of man. But, again, Feuerbach did not develop an ontology in which these terms are central. Nor did he coin the term I–Thou. Gabriel Marcel also testified, in an essay that lauds Buber's thinking and originality, that he himself had "discovered the particular reality of the *Thou* at approximately the same time that Buber was writing his book [*I and Thou*]."[15] What is more, Marcel discovered "the particular reality of the Thou" while he was working on ontological and metaphysical problems. Yet, again, Marcel did not coin the term I–Thou; nor did he use the term in his writings during the 1920s.

But in his lectures in 1927 and 1928 Heidegger attacked specifically the term I–Thou. Consequently, the historical evidence currently at our disposal clearly indicates that, when Heidegger rejected the I–Thou on ontological grounds, he could only have been relating to a term that was coined in *I and Thou* by Martin Buber.

* * *

The disagreement between Heidegger and Buber over the status of the I–Thou becomes more complex and problematic when we note that the two above brief citations from Heidegger and Buber—in which they criticize each other's fundamental thinking—are false. It is false to state, as Heidegger does without proving it, that you cannot recognize the I–Thou relationship existentially, if you do not ask what existence means. Great literature, such as that of Leo Tolstoy and Ernest Hemingway, and many biographical sources, suggest that many people who never read or thought about the meaning of existence have recognized the unique encounter that Buber called the I–Thou relationship. It is also false, and can only be attributed to a very selective or superficial reading of Heidegger's many enlightening texts, to hold, as Buber did, that "Heidegger's self is *a closed system.*" Many details and insights from the writings of Heidegger and Buber, which emerge in the following chapters, show that both these citations are erroneous. But these details are not immediately necessary, because even a first reading of the major texts of these authors, Heidegger's *Being and Time* and Buber's *I and Thou*, suffices to reveal the errors.

Furthermore, in the decades that have passed since the false statements were written, many thinkers and scholars have situated both Buber and Heidegger at the forefront of existential thinking. Their writings are repeatedly read, taught in universities, and discussed in meetings of scholars. Hence, there is a need to clarify the disagreement between these seminal thinkers. At this point, with the scant wisdom we gain with hindsight, I can state: Both false statements, that of Heidegger and that of Buber, seem to be an attempt to rudely dismiss the basic insights and thoughts of a person whose thinking seem to create a problem for one's own thinking. False as these cited statements may be, they do not diminish the fact that there is a profound ontological disagreement between Heidegger and Buber.

Today, therefore, the careful reader of the works of these two thinkers will encounter three immediate questions concerning the I–Thou that demand one's attention: What is the ontological status of the I–Thou? Do Heidegger's many enlightening insights that emerge in his fundamental ontology, insights that contributed much to twentieth-century philosophy, cast doubts upon the I–Thou that Buber articulately described? Is Buber's criticism of Heidegger's fundamental ontology, in which he argues that it ignores a major dimension of human existence that includes the I–Thou, valid? These major questions will be addressed in this book. The examination rising from these questions, I believe, will illuminate many basic problems of ontology; it will also help us to understand the core of Heidegger's and Buber's thinking.

It should be kept in mind that responding to these three questions has more than strict philosophical significance, because both Buber and Heidegger pointed to a way of living a worthy life. Indeed, for both thinkers, the status of the I–Thou has implications for personal existence and a person's existence in society. Some of these implications appear in the chapters that follow. Here we can state in abbreviated manner some major differences that may appear at first reading.

The worthy life that Buber repeatedly extolled includes an emphasis on interhuman relations, specifically genuine dialogue, and those moments of grace which he called I–Thou encounters. Such a life does not seem to have included thinking in detail about the Being of beings, or action in the political realm. For Heidegger, a worthy life included authenticity, facing one's own death resolutely, and in his later writings, dwelling poetically, and learning to be the shepherd of Being. It did not include genuine dialogue or political activities in which you may pursue justice. Nor did the worthy life, as emphasized by Heidegger, include the wholeness that Buber described as emerging in genuine dialogue, and in moments of love and friendship. Wholeness for Heidegger emerges in a different context—in facing one's death authentically. A major chapter of *Being and Time* is called "Dasein's Possibility of Being-a-Whole, and Being-Toward-Death."[16] In contrast to discovering one's wholeness through relating to one's own death, Buber's writings suggest that in the I–Thou encounter, I relate as a whole being to the whole being of the other who is my partner in this moment of dialogue.

Note, however, that the concepts of wholeness and authenticity and other concepts that I have presented are still rather abstract and seem remote. To relate wisely to the controversy between Buber and Heidegger, these concepts must be made intelligible and concrete. I shall strive to do so in the following chapters, often by bringing examples from literature. Put differently, since this book deals with an ontological controversy between two existentialists, each of whom on the basis of his understanding of ontology pointed to a worthy way of life, it is fitting that I endeavor to ground my thoughts and findings in situations and events of everyday existence. Concrete examples are important for making vivid and clear the profound thoughts and the wisdom on human existence presented by both thinkers—thoughts and wisdom which are often expressed very abstractly.

But finding such examples is no simple task. Buber's and Heidegger's writings do not present many vivid specific examples that could clarify their abstract thoughts. The opposite may often seem true; both thinkers, frequently, seem to shy away from concrete examples and from being specific. Concerning Buber's vague writings, Jochanan Bloch once correctly remarked:

Buber had a lifelong tendency for lack of specificity. A kind of conceptual abstraction prevailed in him, which shied away from a specific commandment, specific contents, and if you like—from the crudeness of life, with its burdens, its materialistic and rigidified element, its cruelty.[17]

Bloch's remark about Buber's lack of specificity is true, as will be seen in later chapters of this book. What is more, very frequently, such lack of specifity is also true of Heidegger's writings. A kind of conceptual abstraction prevails in his books also. In the realm of existentialism, however, such conceptual abstraction is not necessary. Søren Kierkegaard, Gabriel Marcel, Jean-Paul Sartre, Simone de Beauvoir, Albert Camus, and other existentialists wrote literature, drama, and also philosophical essays in which, quite often, conceptual abstraction is supported by concrete examples. Indeed, in their philosophical writings, these thinkers often presented living examples that helped make their thinking specific and concrete. Buber and Heidegger are much less forthcoming in providing concrete examples that support their thinking.

What about Buber's Hasidic tales, and his writings on the Hasidic community? Don't they provide concrete examples of lives lived in accordance with Buber's wisdom? With some hesitation, I do not fully agree. At best, Buber's writings on Hasidism and his retelling of Hasidic tales contribute only partially to mitigating his conceptual abstractions. In the chapters of this book, I cite not one Hasidic tale to support or clarify a concept proffered by Buber. But I have found writings by William Shakespeare, Marcel Proust, Leo Tolstoy, and other great writers to be very helpful in providing concrete examples for rather abstract ideas that have been formulated by both Heidegger and Buber. Thus, an additional task that emerged in dealing with the Heidegger–Buber controversy was finding the concrete examples that clarify each thinker's thoughts and insights.

* * *

In order to respond to the question concerning the ontological status of the I–Thou, the first seven chapters of this book will describe the ontology that Heidegger presented in detail in the late 1920s. These chapters will also examine and discuss Heidegger's reasons for rejecting the I–Thou. In the following four chapters I'll briefly describe Buber's ontological writings and findings and examine and discuss his reasons for rejecting Heidegger's fundamental ontology. In the final chapter, I point to additional ontological challenges, beyond the conclusions that I have reached in this study. While following my detailed examinations and discussions, the reader should keep in mind a major difference between Heidegger and Buber. Although the ontology of Heidegger shares many perspectives with that of Buber, they were developed independently and commence from a different starting point.

Consider a few passages that already testify to the differences between Heidegger's and Buber's approach to ontology. On the first page of *Being and Time*, Heidegger sets out the goal of his study: "So it is fitting that we should raise anew *the question of the meaning of Being*."[18] This goal, I should add, was central to Heidegger's thinking throughout his life. The first page of *I and Thou* attempts to elucidate the twofold world established by each person. "To man the world is twofold, in accordance with his twofold attitude."[19] This twofoldness emerges, Buber holds, in a person's possibility to speak the primary word I–Thou, or the primary word I–It. In this book, I will follow each thinker's ideas, as they evolve from these different starting points, so as to reach and to present their ideas on ontology.

Even after a brief encounter with their basic texts, one notices a major distinction between the ontological thinking of Heidegger and Buber: each thinker drew on different sources in developing his thought on beings. Heidegger learned much from early Greek philosophy; he repeatedly explained that the question of the meaning of Being was first raised lucidly and poignantly by the pre-Socratic philosophers: Heraclitus, Anaximander, Parmenides, and others. He believed that even today much can and should be learned from the philosophical fragments that we have and are attributed to these thinkers. Heidegger also was very well versed in the thinking of many Western philosophers, from Plato to Edmund Husserl and Max Scheler. He lectured on the thinking of Plato, Aristotle, Immanuel Kant, Friedrich von Schelling, Gottfried Leibnitz, Friedrich Nietzsche, and many others. These lecture courses were later published as books in his collected writings. It seems that Heidegger's careful reading of these philosophers helped him in his quest to raise anew the question of the meaning of Being, and to attempt to respond to that question in his thinking on ontology and on human existence.

Buber was also well versed in Western philosophy. However, his thinking and writing do not draw as much from this philosophical tradition as did Heidegger. It does not seem to be the primary major source for Buber's thinking about ontology. It is evident that Buber's Jewish heritage, and his research on the Bible, on Hasidism, and on other Jewish topics also influenced many aspects of his thinking. Often relying upon this heritage, Buber repeatedly stressed the importance of human relationships and human encounters, as exemplifying and explicating the ontological thinking that underlies *I and Thou*, and also as serving to clarify his thinking on the significance of human dialogue.

To be faithful to each thinker, the chapters of this book separately present Heidegger's and Buber's thoughts on ontology and the implications of their thinking. I will also briefly show, albeit not always explicitly and in detail, that the disagreements emerging from these two ontological approaches led to a major difference in the views of Heidegger and Buber on what is a worthy life. A few major and profound differences, it will turn out, stem from each thinker's view on the ontological status of the I–Thou and from the value and significance that he attributed to this relationship in human existence.

As indicated, throughout his life much of Heidegger's thinking was addressed to responding to the question of the meaning of Being. He repeatedly stated that to respond to this question he must develop a fundamental ontology of Dasein, the human entity. This fundamental ontology of Dasein needs very careful elaboration in order to perceive the reasons that Heidegger rejected the I–Thou. In what follows, I dedicate three chapters to *Being and Time,* Heidegger's masterpiece. The following four chapters are dedicated to the lecture courses, which were published later, in which he rejected the I–Thou.

In passing, I should add that this book will not relate to Martin Heidegger's well-published adherence to Nazism during the 1930s and early 1940s. I will not examine the views and statements that Heidegger expressed in support of Nazism, nor discuss the relation of these views to his other writings. I recognize that this important topic has concerned many prominent scholars for two decades. In another study of Heidegger's thinking, I have explained in some detail that, despite Heidegger's many evil and despicable acts in supporting Nazism, there is much to be learned from his thinking. I still believe this approach to be true.[20]

* * *

In contrast to Heidegger, Buber did not dedicate much of his thinking and scholarly life to discussing and clarifying basic ontological questions. I do not remember a text in which he raises the question of Being. From 1923 on, he primarily wanted to point to the I–Thou, to a dialogical life, and to elucidate the significance of the I–Thou and of dialogical existence. He often relied on the intuitions of his readers to grasp his thinking. It is true that after the publication of *I and Thou* he wrote essays which addressed ontological problems. Yet, unlike Heidegger, Buber did not struggle to develop an encompassing ontology of human existence. Furthermore, during his long life, Buber undertook other major scholarly endeavors, such as translating the Hebrew Bible into German and pointing to the significance of the Hasidic community as a religious-communal example of worthy existence. I should add that some of Buber's ontological insights emerge briefly, in writings that do not necessarily deal with philosophical questions or with ontology.

Since Buber did not deal much with ontology, my discussion of his ontological thought requires less space. Chapters 8 and 9 present Buber's ontological thinking as presented in *I and Thou* and his view of the I–Thou relationship. Chapters 10 and 11 present and discuss essays in which his thoughts on ontology and on living a life of genuine dialogue are presented. Some of these essays also hint how a life of genuine dialogue can be realized. In another study, I suggested briefly how these hints, and other ideas that Buber proffered his readers, can help the educator teach persons to realize a life of dialogue.[21]

Once the ontologies of Buber and of Heidegger have been presented and compared, it will be possible to respond to the three questions mentioned above. In the final, concluding chapter, we shall be able to answer clearly the major question that led to this study: What is the ontological status of the I–Thou?

NOTES

1. Martin Heidegger, *The Basic Problems of Phenomenology*, trans. Albert Hofstadter (Bloomington: Indiana University Press, 1982).

2. Ibid., p. 298.

3. Martin Heidegger, *Phenomenological Interpretation of Kant's "Critique of Pure Reason,"* trans. Parvis Emad and Kenneth Maly (Bloomington: Indiana University Press, 1997).

4. Martin Heidegger, *The Metaphysical Foundations of Logic*, trans. Michael Heim (Bloomington: Indiana University Press, 1984).

5. Martin Buber, "What Is Man?" in *Between Man and Man*, trans. Ronald Gregor Smith (Boston: Beacon Press, 1955).

6. Ibid., p. 171.

7. Martin Buber, *Eclipse of God* (New York: Harper & Row, 1952).

8. Otto Poggeler, *Martin Heidegger's Path of Thinking*, trans. Daniel Magurshak and Sigmund Barber (Atlantic Highlands, N.J.: Humanities Press, 1987).

9. Robert E. Wood, *Martin Buber's Ontology: An Analysis of "I and Thou"* (Evanston, Ill.: Northwestern University Press, 1969).

10. Lawrence Vogel, *The Fragile "We": Ethical Implications of Heidegger's "Being and Time"* (Evanston, Ill.: Northwestern University Press, 1994).

11. Ibid., p. 1.

12. Heinrich Ott, "Hermeneutic and Personal Structure of Language," in Joseph J. Kockelmans, ed., *On Heidegger and Language* (Evanston, Ill.: Northwestern University Press, 1972), pp. 169–193.

13. Rivka Horwitz, "Ferdinand Ebner As a Source of Martin Buber's Dialogic Thought in *I and Thou,*" in Haim Gordon and Jochanan Bloch, eds., *Martin Buber: A Centenary Volume* (New York: Ktav, 1984), pp. 121–138.

14. See Martin Buber, "What Is Man?" op. cit., especially the section "Feuerbach and Nietzsche."

15. Gabriel Marcel, "I and Thou," in Paul Arthur Schilpp and Maurice Friedman, eds., *The Philosophy of Martin Buber* (LaSalle, Ill.: Open Court, 1967), p. 41.

16. Martin Heidegger, *Being and Time*, trans. John Macquarrie and Edward Robinson (Oxford, Eng.: Basil Blackwell, 1962), pp. 279–311.

17. Jochanan Bloch, "Opening Remarks," in *Martin Buber: A Centenary Volume*, op. cit., p. xvi.

18. Heidegger, *Being and Time*, op. cit., p. 22.

19. Martin Buber, *I and Thou*, trans. Ronald Gregor Smith (New York: Collier Books, 1987), p. 3.

20. See the Introduction in Haim Gordon, *Dwelling Poetically: Educational Challenges in Heidegger's Thinking on Poetry* (Amsterdam: Rodopi, 2000).

21. Haim Gordon, *Dance, Dialogue, and Despair: Existentialist Philosophy and Education for Peace in Israel* (Tuscaloosa: University of Alabama Press, 1986).

PART I

HEIDEGGER'S FUNDAMENTAL ONTOLOGY OF DASEIN

Section A: Being and Time

Chapter 1

Dasein and the World

Many scholars and thinkers consider *Being and Time* to be Heidegger's masterpiece and a classic of twentieth-century philosophy.[1] I agree with this evaluation. In this seminal work, Heidegger first presented in print key concepts of his philosophy, such as Dasein and Being-in-the-world, and defined his phenomenological approach to addressing the philosophical problems that concerned him. The phenomenological approach first presented in *Being and Time* was central to his thinking throughout his life. Hence, any attempt to understand Heidegger's fundamental ontology must begin with the approach and with the ideas developed in *Being and Time*.

Being and Time opens with a question, with Heidegger's answer to the question, and with a challenge that he poses:

Do we in our time have an answer to the question of what we really mean by the word "being"? Not at all. So it is fitting that we should raise anew *the question of the meaning of Being*.[2]

Responding to this challenge of raising anew the question of the meaning of Being was not a simple undertaking. Much of Heidegger's thinking during his life may be viewed as an attempt to respond to the challenge that he posed in *Being and Time*. While addressing and writing about many philosophical problems, such as the essence of technology, the essence of humanism, the origin of a work of art, or the importance of the poetry of Friedrich Hölderlin, he repeatedly strove to also raise anew the question of the meaning of Being.

In the introduction to *Being and Time*, Heidegger indicates that in order to raise anew the question of the meaning of Being a new approach is needed. Being is not an entity. In everyday life and in philosophical thinking, we are accustomed to raise questions about entities, such as this hammer, Gustav Mahler's Fifth Symphony, or a friend's smile. In everyday discourse, and in most philosophical works, it is almost always entities that are discussed. You will very rarely encounter a person or a thinker who raises the question of the meaning of Being. Nor is nothingness, which is linked to the question of the meaning of Being, a major topic of everyday discourse, or even of philosophical discussion. Thus, Heidegger believes, raising anew the question of the meaning of Being requires an approach that is not confined to the terms of everyday discourse or to the concepts and ideas prevailing in most philosophical discussions.

Heidegger notes that entities can be interrogated about their Being. But in response to such questioning of entities, Being must be exhibited in a unique manner, which is different from the way entities are disclosed. Heidegger asks: Which entity would best provide us with an adequate starting point to raise anew the question of Being? His answer is the human entity, which is the only entity which can raise the question of the meaning of Being and attempt to respond to it. Only the human entity is an inquirer, only a human being is transparent in its own Being and can therefore provide an access to the question of Being. Heidegger denotes the human entity Dasein. *Being and Time* presents the fundamental ontology of Dasein and thus provides a basis for raising, albeit in a roundabout manner, the question of the meaning of Being. This ontology, parts of which I very briefly present, is crucial for understanding Heidegger's views on the status of the I–Thou.

I can already mention, however, that Heidegger's initial description of Dasein, that is, the human entity, as an inquirer, as transparent in its own Being, and as providing an access to the question of Being, partially contradicts Buber's statement, cited in the Introduction to the present study. In that statement, Buber wrote that "Heidegger's self is *a closed system*."[3] It would be extremely difficult to imagine a self that is a closed system which nevertheless persistently inquires about beings, is transparent and provides access to the question of Being. I would add that not even Gottfried Leibnitz's universe, populated by monads who do not communicate with each other, seems to fit the description of a closed system. What is more, Buber's statement concerning Heidegger's self can be immediately termed false when one learns that Heidegger describes the basic state of Dasein as Being-in-the-world, and this state includes Being-with other Daseins in the world.

* * *

Before clarifying Being-in-the-world as the basic state of Dasein, Heidegger points out that he bases his analysis on the everyday way of being of Dasein, on Dasein's everyday activities and concerns. This point will emerge as crucial. At the outset let me only mention that in the everydayness of Dasein that Heidegger, quite often, brilliantly describes, he does not mention some very important human experiences, such as love or friendship. Indeed, this point will repeatedly emerge in the chapters that follow; it is therefore worth emphasizing at the outset: In the many volumes of his published thinking, volumes from which we have much to learn, Heidegger very rarely mentions love or friendship. Nor have I found in these volumes a philosophical discussion of these human relationships such as those found in, say, Plato's *Phaedrus* or in Cicero's *On Friendship*. Hence, the everyday Being-in-the-world of Dasein, which is articulately described in *Being and Time*, frequently tends toward the instrumental, or, if you wish, it often portrays Dasein as a manipulator of equipment. It also reveals that this equipment-oriented Dasein, at times, can relate authentically as a thinker. Such a human existence may often seem quite deficient, especially when compared with the richness of interhuman relations described by thinkers such as Plato, Cicero, and, of course, Martin Buber.

When introducing his newly coined term Being-in-the-world, which has since attained prominence in the writings of not a few other important philosophers—for instance, Jean-Paul Sartre—Heidegger stresses that it stands for a unitary phenomenon. While this phenomenon cannot be broken up into pieces, it does have constitutive items. He mentions three such items, which can be formulated as questions: What is the ontological structure of the world? Who is the entity who is Dasein in its average everydayness, and whose state is Being-in-the-world? What does "Being-in" mean for the human entity, that is, what is the ontological constitution of "inhood" for Dasein? To each of these questions Heidegger devotes a later chapter; however, he immediately gives a preliminary sketch of what "Being-in" means for Dasein.

"Being-in" does not mean the same kind of "in" as when we say that there is milk in the pitcher or that the books stand in the bookcase. Heidegger calls the relation of milk to the pitcher and of the books to the bookcase insideness, which is a spatial relation. The milk is inside the pitcher, the books are inside the bookcase. All those beings whose relation to each other is merely spatial—and these can include huge entities such as buildings, cities, planets, and galaxies—are termed by Heidegger Beings which are present-at-hand. The ontological relations of those entities, which are present-at-hand to each other, he calls categorical—a term which designates the relations between beings which are not Dasein. These relations are categorical because they are defined by external categories.

In contrast, Heidegger calls "Being-in" for Dasein an existentiale. Existentialia denote the character of Being of Dasein. Heidegger thus divorces Dasein from the realm of categories, since the human entity is not an object or a subject. Or as Poggeler puts it:

Just as it [Dasein] is not an object which occurs in the "world" in the totality of beings, neither is it a worldless subject from which one would have to build a bridge to the "world," something that has been tried time and again since Descartes.[4]

Neither an object nor a worldless subject, Dasein exists already as Being-in-the-world, as a being already engaged in the world. Consequently, "Being-in" as an existentiale is a relation which is central to the ontological structure of Dasein's existence.

Heidegger explains that for Dasein "Being-in" relates to dwelling in the world, which is very different from merely being present-at-hand in the world. Dwelling in the world means "Being alongside" the world, absorbed with it and concerned about the world and its beings. Indeed, a major ontological aspect of "Being-in" is that Dasein, as a dweller in the world, helps to establish the world and is concerned with the world. It is evident that no such concern can ever emerge in objects that are present-at-hand, such as quarks, or stones, or buildings, or planets, or black holes, or galaxies. Put differently, the Being of those objects which Heidegger calls categorical does not include relating to a world, or, of course, concern with the world.

Heidegger discusses knowledge in order to exemplify Being-in as a basic mode of Dasein's existence. He rejects the belief that knowledge is a relationship between a human soul and the world, as two entities that are present-at-hand to each other. Such an approach leads to the superficial idea that knowing is primarily a relation between subject and object, which Heidegger admits has some truth to it. But, he immediately adds, the idea is also vacuous, since it ignores the true ontological status of Dasein as Being-in-the-world. He repeatedly stresses that subject and object do not coincide with Dasein and the world. Furthermore, knowing is not present-at-hand in the world, nor is it in some way "inside" the subject. Such approaches to comprehending, clarifying, and defining knowing ignore the question of the Being of knowing. In contrast, Heidegger commences his brief inquiry with the question about the mode of being of knowledge; he reaches the conclusion that "knowing is a mode of Being of Dasein as Being-in-the-world."[5]

He explains. Dasein can produce, manipulate, utilize, and bring changes to entities that it encounters. Such a relating to entities requires a certain type of "knowledge." Yet knowledge, for Heidegger, is primarily Dasein's attempt to determine the nature or the essence of things that are present-at-hand. Such knowledge does not arise solely from manipulating entities and from similar modes of Being-in-the-world. Rather, in order to know the nature of things, Dasein must often detach itself from all forms of manipulating, or of utilizing, an entity and merely perceive it, and think about what it perceives. By such perceiving and thinking, quite often the essence or nature of a being is disclosed.

Knowledge of essences is linked to Dasein's concern and fascination with the world, to Dasein's dwelling in the world, and hence to its "Being alongside" the world. The mode of being which leads to such knowledge requires that Dasein hold itself back from any manipulating or using of the entities present-at-hand about which knowledge is sought. Often, only by such holding back can Dasein perceive the entities in the detached manner that may lead to knowledge. Thus, "Being in" for Dasein includes being concerned with the world and with the essences of the things that exist in it; this concern, however, may lead Dasein to be detached from entities that it meets as it strives to obtain knowledge.

The perception that may lead to knowledge requires that Dasein address itself to a specific thing and discuss it as such, in its uniqueness. However, Heidegger mentions, the addressing and discussing of a thing is always an interpretation which determines the thing. Today, following scientific observation and exploration, the moon is known to be a dark satellite revolving around the earth that reflects the light of the sun. For centuries before Copernicus, however, the moon was recognized as an independent celestial luminary that projected its own light.

Some ancient religions attributed holiness to the moon. Some customs stemming from this holiness are still with us. Orthodox Jews bless the moon at the end of Yom Kippur service. For Moslems, the birth of the moon determines the beginning and end of the month-long fast of Ramadan. Those ancients, and also our contemporaries who view the moon as holy, perceived and still perceive the same moon that we do. Their interpretation differs. Note that these different interpretations did not interfere with the activities of, say, those medieval thinkers who compiled calendars of the year on the basis of their perceptions of the moon. Think of Saadia Gaon, who compiled the Jewish calendar which is still in use. Asserting, as we do today, that the moon is merely a satellite that reflects the light of the sun is the result of our obtaining knowledge through inquiring and our interpreting that knowledge and what we see. Very often, Heidegger would add, we obtain this knowledge while existing alongside the moon and other entities and refraining from any attempt to utilize them.

* * *

In describing the ontological structure of the world, Heidegger first explains that the world is not the collection of all the entities that are present-at-hand. Among these present-at-hand entities, he admits, are things such as diamonds, gold nuggets, and oil fields that Dasein may invest with value; but that does not change their ontological status. Nor is the world a unity of all the entities that are present-at-hand under a concept such as Nature. Indeed, Nature is also one of those entities encountered already in the world by Dasein. When discussing Nature, Dasein has already presupposed the world. Consequently, to grasp the world as a constituent of Being-in-the-world, we must not try to reduce the world to its entities, but rather attempt to bring out of concealment the worldhood of the world. Such a manner of inquiry, of bringing an essence or a truth out from unconcealment, may help to discover the essence of the world.

Like "Being-in," worldhood is not a category, it is an existentiale. It must be brought forth to our comprehension as it emerges in Dasein's everyday existence as Being-in-the-world. To bring forth the worldhood of the world, Heidegger begins from the fact that Dasein is that being whose immediate environment is constituted by the concernful use of equipment. This immediate environment is, of course, part of the world; at least partially this environment also reflects the basic constitution of worldhood. For Heidegger, daily concern in the use of equipment is basic to constituting the world, as Dasein exists in it. Consequently, one way to better comprehend the world in which everyday Dasein exists, is to uncover the kind of Being which equipment possesses. Hence, Heidegger's discussion of worldhood begins with his describing Dasein as a user of equipment. He reminds us: any piece of equipment belongs to the totality of equipment, which is made up of those things which Dasein uses in-order-to. He calls the kind of Being that a piece of equipment possesses readiness-to-hand. This pliers and that pen are ready-to-hand in the drawers of my desk. Note that the term ready-to-hand already hints at a concernful existence.

Each Dasein, in pursuing its unique existence, is always involved with equipment that is ready-to-hand. Dasein utilizes this equipment in-order-to attain specific goals, which accord with what Heidegger denotes a "for-the-sake-of-which" that each Dasein assigns to itself. But Dasein assigns itself to a task from a specific "wherein," with its involvements, which include relations, equipment, signs, references, tasks, and goals. This "wherein" is born of a primordial act of understanding in which one encounters entities "in the kind of Being that belongs to involvements." Heidegger adds: "this 'wherein' is the phenomenon of the world."[6] Thus, Dasein's primordial understanding of itself as Being-in-the-world at a specific "wherein" is a defining constituent of the world-hood of the world.

It is important to point out immediately that Heidegger's beginning with equipment, in order to discuss the worldhood of Dasein as Being-in-the-world, may be problematic. Some very significant features of the human everyday world do not at all stem from the equipmentlike character of worldhood and are not related to those things that Dasein uses in-order-to. From my reading, it seems that in Heidegger's equipment-oriented world there seems to be almost no space for passionate love and its wonderful, often euphoric blessings. Nor does his description of Dasein's everyday world seem to allow for the emergence of Buber's I–Thou relationship. Nor, as we shall repeatedly discover, does Heidegger's equipmentlike world include the space between persons that Buber states is essential for genuine dialogue to come into being. From Heidegger's presentation, it seems quite clear that the Being of love, of friendship, and of genuine dialogue have nothing to do with readiness-to-hand.

Could it be that the everyday concern linked to equipment, which Heidegger describes as central to Dasein's being, narrows human existence? Could it be that Heidegger's description of the worldhood of the world, in which we humans exist, is in many respects spiritually shallow? Answers to these questions slowly emerge in the sequel.

I will not follow all Heidegger's arguments about the way the world announces itself. Suffice to mention his belief that the totality of equipment is central to the constitution of the worldhood of the world, whose context is lit up in certain circumstances. These circumstances may be when a piece of equipment breaks down and the presence-at-hand of entities of the world emerges. The worldhood of my world may also emerge through a sign which refers me to certain pieces of equipment, to other signs, and to the totality of equipment. Indeed, Heidegger describes the worldhood of Dasein's everyday world as constituted of equipment, signs, and references, which merge into a totality whose ultimate reference is Dasein. This description is the opposite extreme, he holds, from Descartes's ontological approach, which describes the world as constituted from extended things that are not linked to Dasein as Being-in-the-world. Skipping his just critique of Descartes, I turn to Heidegger's discussion of spatiality.

* * *

As mentioned, Heidegger holds that Dasein's Being-in is not merely spatial in the way that the milk is *in* the pitcher or the books are *in* the bookcase. Dasein's Being-in is not characterized by insideness, which is a spatial category. The question arises: How does Dasein, as Being-in-the-world, relate to space?

Heidegger responds with an examination of the spatiality of equipment, which already has a closeness to Dasein. Any piece of equipment has its place within Dasein's region of activities, in which other pieces of equipment also have a place. Together, these pieces of equipment exist within a region; they constitute Dasein's context of equipment, and its space of existence. Thus, the three-dimensional Newtonian space of physics, filled with things that are present-at-hand, is not the space encountered by Dasein in its everyday existence. Rather, Newtonian space is veiled in what Heidegger denotes the spatiality of the ready-to-hand, which emerges in a person's everyday life.

Spatiality emerges in Dasein's everydayness because those entities that are ready-to-hand have a place, even if that place changes every moment. The sun's place is evident; it is ready-to-hand daily in the sky above me with uniform constancy, even if its place in the heavens changes continually, from hour to hour and from season to season. The place of the sun also determines the character of places of other entities—there is the sunny side of the house in the morning and the shady area of the goldfish pool in the afternoon. Heidegger's point is that the world in which Dasein is involved reveals spatiality through the places of those entities that are ready-to-hand, that is, through the involvement of Dasein with entities and with their specific places in its constituted world. Consequently, he denotes Dasein as "spatial" in relation to its Being-in-the-world.

Dasein's spatiality, however, is not similar to the spatiality of entities that are ready-to-hand or present-at-hand. Its spatiality is not characterized by a specific place, or by being at a certain position in world space, or even by being in Einsteinian space-time. Dasein's spatiality, Heidegger holds, is characterized by what he calls de-severence and directionality, which are ways by which Dasein is involved spatially in the world. By de-severence he means making the farness of an entity disappear, by bringing it close to me. Looking at Jupiter through a telescope is an act of de-severence, as is watching an airplane land on the runway, or locating the number of a house that I am seeking.

Dasein is essentially de-severent—it lets any entity, whatever its distance, be encountered as close by. De-severence is an existentiale; as such it implies no explicit estimate of the distance between Dasein and the entity ready-to-hand. Despite its great distance from earth—a distance that can be determined by astronomers—when Dasein studies Jupiter through a telescope, Jupiter becomes close to Dasein's being, often closer than the mirror of the telescope. Heidegger holds that Dasein has an essential tendency toward closeness, hence it is constantly concerned with finding ways of de-severing the entities in the world. The Internet is a recently developed mediator by which what appears on a screen has, seemingly, already been de-severed for Dasein's benefit. The widespread use of the Internet may serve as an example of Dasein's tendency to find ways of making entities in the world closer to its being. Note, however, that there is often an element of illusion in the closeness of entities that are presented to Dasein, for instance, when looking through a telescope or when watching the screen of a personal computer.

The specific acts of de-severing of each Dasein constitute the real world for it. Put differently, the space of the world that each Dasein exists alongside is very much determined by its specific acts of de-severing. The space of the world alongside which exists a person who is addicted to scanning the Internet will be very different from the space of the world alongside which an outdoor botanist exists. And both personal spaces differ significantly from that of the astronomer studying Jupiter with a telescope.

Consequently, Dasein's everyday spatiality has little to do with Newtonian space, or, for that matter, with Einsteinian space-time. These so-called scientific concepts of space, which help to lay the foundation of physical sciences, relate primarily to things that are present-at-hand. The physical concepts of space relate only externally to a being such as Dasein, who understands its being here, in this place, in relation to a specific environment of the world, populated by entities that it de-severs. These concepts also relate externally to the elements of Dasein's specific environment, which includes regions and contexts of equipment. Heidegger states that Dasein discovers space by virtue of the fact that it "constantly comports itself de-severently towards the entities thus spatially encountered."[7] Indeed, Dasein does not initially discover space through the abstract mathematical thinking that is needed to grasp Newton's or Einstein's concepts.

Directionality is also characteristic of the Being-in of Dasein and of its everyday de-severings. Each de-severing of an entity is already directed toward a region that concerns Dasein as Being-in-the-world. De-severing Jupiter with the aid of a telescope is directed toward a much different region than de-severing the opera *Moses and Aaron* by Arnold Schönberg while seated in the Deutsche Opera House in Berlin; and both regions differ from the region de-severed by an army officer who is planning an attack on an enemy fortification. Heidegger concludes his presentation of Dasein's relation to space with two statements: space is not in the subject; nor is the world in space.

Heidegger probably presents the first statement because some thinkers and scholars, after reading Kant, seem to have inferred that space is in the subject. He also rejects the idea that the world is moving in infinite space, as some of the models emerging from prevailing physical theories seem to suggest. The foundation of space is a result of the fact that Dasein is spatial as Being-in-the-world. Dasein's de-severing and direction-ality daily bear testimony to its spatiality and also establish the regions of space that constitute Dasein's world.

Of course, it is probably more than three millennia since humans first trod the path of scientific thinking along which the homogeneous space of the sciences was discovered and discussed. Such a discovery and dis-cussion, Heidegger explains, requires disregarding the realm of the ready-to-hand and the specific regions of space that, taken together, constitute Dasein's environment and establish its world. This homoge-neous space, which became the metrical space of physics, cosmology, and the physical sciences—this scientific space that was developed over the centuries—becomes evident to Dasein only by depriving the entities which are ready-to-hand of their worldhood.

Let me stress this point. The space of cosmology and physics comes into being by Dasein's act of depriving beings that are ready-to-hand of their worldhood. I would assert that recent developments within physics in the twentieth century, particularly the "scientific revolution" that led from Newtonian space to Einsteinian space-time and to Werner Heisen-berg's uncertainty principle, very much accords with Heidegger's onto-logical understanding of Dasein's relation to space. But even partially proving this assertion would take us too far afield. Heidegger adds that the Being of space has still not been elucidated; such an elucidation would require a better clarification of the possibilities of Being. Heideg-ger's thinking on space in *Being and Time* goes no further in this direc-tion.[8]

Note, however, that Heidegger's discussion of space as linked to the ready-to-hand and to the present-at-hand does not mention an important dimension—the space of dialogue that can emerge between persons. Bu-ber denotes this space "the between." Later chapters will explain that Buber holds that "the between" is central, and even crucial, for living a life of dialogue. He also indicates that, frequently, a person who lives in a manner that allows for "the between" to come into being may be much more open to the possibility of an I–Thou encounter.

* * *

Heidegger asks: Who is Dasein in its everydayness? As Being-in-the-world, Dasein is that being who is fascinated with the world. Yet to present a more detailed and adequate answer to the question, Heidegger examines two structures of Dasein that are equiprimordial with Being-in-the-world: Being-with and Dasein-with. The need to examine these structures is important because of a prevailing conceptual and perceptual mistake. While Dasein is the entity which I am, in everyday discourse, the "I" or the "Self" or, for that matter, Dasein, are frequently tacitly grasped as entities that are present-at-hand. But, Heidegger stresses, such a manner of conceiving or understanding Dasein is wrong. Presence-at-hand is definitely the kind of Being of entities whose character is *not* that of my Self. Put succinctly, the character of the Being of Dasein is not presence-at-hand, hence the "Who" of Dasein will never be disclosed by relating to it as a being that is present-at-hand. Heidegger concludes that a different approach is required to answer the question Who is Dasein? A phenomenological presentation of the kind of Being that Dasein possesses will help to answer the question.

The who of everyday Dasein does not only relate to equipment or to Nature, that is, to things that are either ready-to-hand or present-at-hand. Dasein also relates to other Daseins, to beings that are like Dasein—they "exist there" like Dasein, and also exist with Dasein. These other Daseins are not necessarily those whom Dasein confronts and stands out against. Rather, in most instances, Dasein exists with these Others in the world and, on the ontological level, does not distinguish itself from them. Put otherwise, Dasein's concernful Being-in-the-world always exists in a world shared with Others, with those beings who exist as Dasein, but Dasein does not necessarily meet each of these individual Daseins. Heidegger formulates this situation thus: Dasein is essentially Being-with. Yet Being-with does not require that the Other be physically present or perceived. We all know that Being-with another person can often be most acute when he or she is absent, say, when you long to be with a loved one, or when you read a letter from a friend. And, in contrast, I can feel painfully alone in a crowd, when surrounded by persons who are totally indifferent to my Being-in-the-world.

Encountering the Other is, therefore, not a meeting of two seemingly indifferent entities that are present-at-hand for each other. Rather, Dasein encounters the Other as coming out of the world that is Dasein's concern. Furthermore, in everyday existence we meet Others primarily in their Being-in-the-world, and we relate to them as such. Of course, I can pass a soldier standing tensely on guard at the entrance to a government building, ignore his Being-in-the-world, and relate to him as if he were a wooden post that is merely present-at-hand. But in my daily relations with most of the Others whom I encounter, I do relate to each Dasein as Being-in-the-world. When I relate thus, I encounter the Other as Dasein-with. When I relate to the soldier on guard as if he were a wooden post, I am alienating him as a Dasein-with. When I feel alone in a crowd it is because the members of the crowd relate indifferently to me and to my Dasein-with. Literary examples support Heidegger's distinctions. When Marcel longs for his grandmother, in Marcel Proust's *Remembrance of Things Past*, and remembers her loving him, it is because Marcel misses her Being-in-the-world; hence longing is Marcel's existing as Dasein-with his grandmother.

Heidegger now distinguishes between concern and solicitude. He coins a specific meaning for each term in the context of Dasein's Being-in-the-world. Both concern and solicitude are manifestations of the phenomenon of care, which is central to Dasein's existence. Concern characterizes Dasein's relationship to equipment, that is, to things that are ready-to-hand. Solicitude characterizes Dasein's relationship to beings who are also Dasein. What exactly does he mean by solicitude?

To answer this question, Heidegger points to what he terms the two extreme possibilities of solicitude, between which all other acts of solicitude are arrayed, seemingly, on a continuum. He only defines these extreme possibilities of solicitude and does not give literary examples or examples from life that would clarify them; nor does he give any examples of solicitude that exist between the two extreme possibilities. Heidegger claims that presenting such descriptions and classifications are beyond the limits of his investigation.

One extreme possibility of solicitude is to take away the Other's care, and to act instead of the Other. Heidegger calls this possibility to *leap in* for the Other. You must remember that Heidegger holds that the totality of Being-in-the-world, as a structural whole, is care. Hence, such solicitude, which takes away the Other's care by leaping in for the Other, limits or curtails or perhaps even partially destroys the structural whole of the Other's Being-in-the-world. In this solicitude, the Other is frequently dominated by, or becomes dependent upon, the Dasein who has leaped in for him or her. Heidegger indicates that this extreme possibility of solicitude, which is very common, is frequently linked to Dasein's relation to equipment. Thus, the passengers of a commercial aircraft depend upon the solicitude of the pilot and the crew to fly them to their destination.

I should add that such solicitude can also deny freedom to the Other, when, for instance, it exists in the political realm. A dictator will dominate his or her subjects by almost always acting instead of them—except, perhaps, when he calls upon them to go to fight in a war. Joseph Stalin, Adolf Hitler, Benito Mussolini, Augusto Pinochet, Francisco Franco, and many other twentieth-century evil dictators never consulted the citizens of the countries that they ruled. Consequently, the Being-in-the-world of persons who are citizens ruled by a wicked dictatorial regime includes very little freedom. Their daily lives are very much dominated by evil rulers and by their many pernicious supporters, who daily engage in the solicitude of leaping in.

Heidegger terms the other extreme possibility of solicitude to *leap ahead* of the Other. In such a leaping ahead, Dasein relates to this specific Other's potentiality-for-being, not in order to take away a person's care, but rather to give it back to him or her, so that he or she can live it authentically for the first time. Thus, solicitude which leaps ahead liberates the Other to be fully itself. This solicitude relates to the existence of this specific Other, and not, say, to the equipment that concerns him or her in everyday engagements. Such solicitude, Heidegger points out, helps this Other become transparent to itself as a Being-in-the-world whose structural whole is care; and it thus assists this Other to become free to live his or her care as authentically as possible.

The educational relationship that Fyodor Dostoyevsky describes in *The Brothers Karamazov*, between Father Zosima, the elder, and Alyosha Karamazov, is an example of solicitude in which Dasein leaps ahead of the Other. (As noted, Heidegger gives no examples of solicitude.) Father Zosima relates with wisdom to Alyosha's potentiality-for-being, carefully and lovingly instructing him what to do so that he can live what Heidegger would call an authentic life of care. Alyosha responds with deep love and strict obedience to Father Zosima's solicitude.

Yet, Dostoyevsky warns, giving yourself, as a student, to the solicitude of a personal educator, in this case an elder, who leaps ahead of you, is no simple commitment. Such a giving of yourself will not necessarily lead to freedom. Here is his description of the religious institution of elders.

What, then is an elder? An elder is one who takes your soul, your will into his soul and into his will. Having chosen an elder, you renounce your will and give it to him under total obedience and with total self-renunciation. A man who dooms himself to this trial, to this terrible school of life, does so voluntarily, in the hope that after the long trial he will achieve self-conquest, self-mastery to such a degree that he will, finally, through a whole life's obedience, attain to perfect freedom—that is freedom from himself—and avoid the lot of those who live their whole lives without finding themselves in themselves. . . . It is also true, perhaps, that this tested and already thousand-year-old instrument for the moral regeneration of man from slavery to freedom and to moral perfection may turn into a double-edged weapon, which may lead a person not to humility and ultimate self-control but, on the contrary, to the most satanic pride—that is to fetters and not to freedom.[9]

On the basis of Dostoyevsky's description of the institution of elders, in which the elder, by leaping ahead of his ward, is supposed to lead him to an enlightened freedom, certain questions should be posed: Are the two poles of solicitude that Heidegger describes indeed distinct? Will it not happen at times, as Dostoyevsky suggests, that leaping ahead of the Other may metamorphose into a leaping in for the Other? Is not Heidegger's description lacking because he does not show the dynamic situation that occurs between the two persons who participate in solicitude—the person who leaps ahead of the Other, or leaps in for the Other, and that specific Other? Indeed, can one correctly and adequately describe and define solicitude, as Heidegger has attempted to do, without describing the dynamic that develops between the participants and without mentioning the dialectical relationship that may often emerge between the two persons participating in the relationship?

We still lack the knowledge of all Heidegger's thinking during this period, which should enable us to answer these questions fully. Posing the questions, in any event, indicates that Heidegger's presentation of solicitude seems to be unable to cope with certain grave problems emerging from Dostoyevsky's thinking.

Heidegger's limited presentation of solicitude, however, is most significant to evaluating his fundamental ontology. Hence, I should add the following three questions, which are intimately linked to the ontological status of the I–Thou and its relation to solicitude: Does Heidegger's description of solicitude help us to comprehend and understand what happens in true love and genuine friendship, relations that Dostoyevsky and other great authors have described and many people have experienced? Can we summarize these wonderful human relations as merely a mutual leaping ahead, or a mutual solicitude? My answer to these two questions is: No.

Hence, my third question: Is it therefore not true that the relations of true love, say between Romeo and Juliet, and genuine friendship, say between Socrates and Plato, transcend, and consequently defy, Heidegger's concept of solicitude? My answer is that these relations indeed transcend Heidegger's concept of solicitude.

Heidegger does sense the complexity of Being-with. He points out that the world that Dasein establishes does not only free the equipment which Dasein utilizes. It also endows Dasein and the Others, the other persons encountered in the world, with freedom. Since the choice of the way to exist one's Being with is a central issue for Dasein, and since Being with belongs to the Being of Dasein, he concludes that, as Being-with, Dasein is essentially for-the-sake-of-others. Solicitude is at the core of Dasein's being, and the choice of the manner of its living solicitude is up to each Dasein. These proclamations, and perhaps a few additional statements, might lead the reader to believe that Heidegger has, perhaps, provided an initial foundation for a response to the above questions concerning love and friendship.

As you continue to read *Being and Time*, however, you discover that Heidegger goes no further than these proclamations in the direction posed by the above questions. He does point out that empathy and Dasein's projection of its self are not ontologically prior and therefore cannot assist in providing a foundation for solicitude. But *Being and Time* does not provide a foundation, on the basis of solicitude, for wonderful human relations such as love and friendship. Nor does it present any thoughts on the dynamics of solicitude, or of interhuman relations, that might help the reader reach a better understanding of Being-with. As Richard Polt observed, "Heidegger gives us some promising hints of a phenomenology of human relationships—only to abandon the project as soon as it is begun."[10]

Instead of pursuing the ideas suggested by his "promising hints" concerning the phenomenology of Being-with, Heidegger abandons the quest. He turns again to the question Who is Dasein in its everydayness? His immediate answer is that in its everyday Being-with toward Others, Dasein is not itself. This answer leads him to present and to describe the role of the "They" [das Man].

* * *

Although Dasein strives to distance itself from Others, and to differ from the Other, Heidegger holds that primarily Dasein is subject to Others. The Others, who are always there in everyday Being-with-one-another determine much of the answer to the question: Who is Dasein in its everydayness? Indeed, in everyday Being-with-one-another Dasein is frequently dissolved completely into the kind of Being that is determined by the Others. Dasein works at jobs that Others work, reads the newspapers that the Others read, rides in the trains that they ride, reads the books that they find interesting to discuss, and finds shocking what they find shocking. Thus, the "They" prescribes the everyday Being of Dasein.

Heidegger concedes that living the everyday Being prescribed by the "They" does not bring honor or integrity to Dasein. Such an everyday Being will not include the great achievements that noble persons have struggled for and obtained. It excludes the possibility of glory that certain persons in history have attained through struggling for things that are worthy, such as beauty, wisdom, or justice. Think of Socrates or of Brutus. How could it be otherwise, since averageness is an existential characteristic of the "They"? Because the ideas and the behavior of the "They" are an expression and an embracing of averageness, the "They" persistently dismisses, disparages, or disregards many things that are outstanding and unique in human existence. Hence the "They" supports an essential, yet ruinous, tendency of Dasein. Heidegger calls this tendency the leveling down of all possibilities of Being. The "They" encourages a mediocre life and always speaks with the banal voice of mediocrity.

Together with this leveling down of all possibilities of Being comes a flight from personal responsibility. Such occurs because the "They" influences every decision, yet it seemingly slips away when a person needs to reach a decision. To see the truth in Heidegger's ontological description, you need only perceive some of the paradigms developed by and used by many sociologists, economists, psychologists, anthropologists, and other social scientists. These paradigms always cite specific social or psychological reinforcements, incentives, or other influences as reasons for a person's decisions. If asked, the social and behavioral scientists who adhere to these paradigms will state that, in all instances, the person decides. But if you look closer at these paradigms, you discover the force of the underlying tenet that states that there are always explainable reasons for each personal decision.

To repeat, the tenet holds that each Dasein's decision is merely a response to reinforcements, incentives, and similar influences. I will not cast doubt upon this rather dubious tenet or upon the paradigms that have been founded upon it. I will say that the influences that it describes are, in most instances, those which the "They" encourages each Dasein to accept as valid guides for its everyday way of life—influences such as money, power, pleasure, and fame. The result of these social scientific paradigms is, therefore, that you can present each Dasein's decision as a result of the guidance of the "They." Yet, even while presenting this approach, the "They" slips away from taking responsibility for that personal decision; it can slip away because, as mentioned, despite their tenet, the social scientists state that the person decides.

Dasein, however, has also learned from this deceptive situation how to evade responsibility. When questioned, Dasein points to specific incentives, reinforcements, and other influences as leading to its decision. Thus, Dasein disburdens itself from assuming responsibility and insidiously shifts the responsibility for its decisions to the "They." When such thinking and everyday leveling down prevail, the result is that, as Heidegger states, "no one" is responsible; and, furthermore, Dasein has surrendered itself to being a "nobody" in its Being-with-one-another. He adds that such a way of life, in which you fail to affirm your self, is inauthentic. At the same time, you cannot fully efface the "They" and its ruinous influence. It is primordial, real, and belongs to what Heidegger calls "Dasein's positive constitution."[11]

It is therefore no surprise that Heidegger distinguishes between the they-self and the authentic-self. In the former, Dasein is dispersed into the "They," and the "They" prescribes its way of relating to the world. To reach the authentic-self, Dasein must clear away all these prescriptions, many of which serve as disguises of reality and of one's self.

* * *

I shall close this chapter by pointing to a literary example that pretty much supports and clarifies Heidegger's concepts. Jean-Paul Sartre's novel *Nausea* describes the process wherein the protagonist, Roquentin, slowly emerges from dispersion into the "They." Roquentin emerges from this dispersion by persistently clearing away the prescriptions of the "They," which insidiously disguise reality and the world that he supposedly encounters. Indeed, as the novel proceeds Roquentin slowly modifies his relation to the "They" and becomes much more an authentic-self.[12]

But, looking at the example of Roquentin, I would add an insight supported by my personal experience. Unmasking the manifestations of the "They," as Roquentin does relentlessly, is not the only path leading to an authentic-self. An authentic existence also may come into being, albeit slowly, when a person strives to engage in dialogical relationships with genuine partners. This path to an authentic existence is firmly supported by Buber's writings, by works of great literature, and by many personal testimonies. Consequently, is not Heidegger's description of Dasein overly monological?

NOTES

1. Martin Heidegger, *Being and Time*, trans. John Macquarrie and Edward Robinson (Oxford, Eng.: Basil Blackwell, 1962).

2. Ibid., p. 21.

3. Martin Buber, *Between Man and Man*, trans. Ronald Gregor Smith (Boston: Beacon Press, 1955), p. 171.

4. Otto Poggeler, *Martin Heidegger's Path of Thinking*, trans. Daniel Magurshak and Sigmund Barber (Atlantic Highlands, N.J.: Humanities Press, 1987), p. 39.

5. Heidegger, *Being and Time*, p. 88.

6. Ibid., p. 119.

7. Ibid., p. 143.

8. Heidegger *did* think about the Being of space during this period. Some of his thoughts on this topic are found in his book *Kant and the Problem of Metaphysics*, first published in 1929. One should also consult his series of lectures for the winter semester 1927–1928, which was published close to five decades later as *Phenomenological Interpretation of Kant's "Critique of Pure Reason."* I discuss both books in later chapters, but not Heidegger's ideas on space.

9. Fyodor Dostoyevsky, *The Brothers Karamazov*, trans. Richard Pevear and Larissa Volokhonsky (New York: Vintage, 1991), pp. 27–29.

10. Richard Polt, *Heidegger: An Introduction* (London: UCL Press, 1999), p. 61.

11. Heidegger, *Being and Time*, p. 167.

12. Jean-Paul Sartre, *Nausea*, trans. Robert Baldick (London: Penguin, 1963).

Chapter 2

Dasein's Being-in, Care, and Truth

Dasein, which we can translate as Being-there, exists at a specific "there." To clarify in greater depth Dasein's Being-in, Heidegger elucidates the existential constitution and the everyday Being of the "Da" of Dasein, that is, of the "there" of the human entity. Dasein's specific "there" points to both a here and a yonder, as does the word *there* which can mean both here and yonder. Furthermore, the "here" of a person is always in relation to a yonder that is ready-to-hand.

Consider the airline pilot during a flight, who from the cockpit of his plane, which is a moving "here," relates to the yonder control tower as ready-to-hand to guide the plane. Since the existential spatiality of each Dasein determines its location, which is grounded upon its Being-in-the-world, most passengers do not concern themselves with the pilot's here and yonder. The airline pilot's location is 18,000 feet above the Pacific Ocean, 350 kilometers from the control tower. As a coach passenger on board, I am located five rows from the movie screen and forty-five minutes from the termination of my flight. Thus, each Dasein, as Being-there, discloses spatiality and enlightens the specific "there" where it exists and relates to other beings.

Dasein is always "there" in a state of mind or mood which discloses how it is, and how it encounters something that matters in the world. My mood is joyful at breakfast with my lovely wife; a half-hour later I am enraged when reading in the newspaper reports of Israeli violations of the Palestinians' human rights. Precisely these moods bring Being to my being "there"—at the breakfast table or at my desk reading the newspaper. Of course, I may curb my rage and not give in to my mood. Equanimity is also a mood. Yet, even if I become master of my moods, I cannot deny that, ontologically, moods are a primordial kind of Being. Thrown into its "there," Dasein finds itself in the mood that it has. Dasein is never free of moods. Each mood that assails it discloses Dasein's Being-in-the-world as a whole.

Heidegger adds that even if Dasein has a clear direction in its life and knows its "whence" and "whither," Dasein's moods are an enigma. It is not at all clear why certain moods assail Dasein at any given time, nor is it clear why these moods arise out of its specific Being-in-the-world. States of mind are also an enigma, because even though Dasein's mood discloses its Being-in-the-world as a whole, by being in a mood, Dasein frequently evades its very self.

Heidegger's discussion of fear, as an illustration of a state of mind, later helps him to distinguish fear from anxiety. In his distinction between fear and anxiety, he pretty much follows the insights of Søren Kierkegaard, who wrote:

The concept of anxiety is almost never treated in psychology. Therefore, I must point out that it is altogether different from fear and similar concepts that refer to something definite, whereas anxiety is freedom's actuality as the possibility of possibility. For this reason, anxiety is not found in the beast, precisely because by nature the beast is not qualified as spirit.[1]

Dasein's being "there" is maintained not only by moods. Equiprimordial with its states of mind is Dasein's understanding, which, on the everyday level of existence, is linked to its for the sake of which. Understanding is an existentiale. Heidegger calls understanding that disclosure of Being-in-the-world as such which is grounded upon Dasein's for-the-sake-of-which. An airline pilot who daily strives to excel discloses a Being-in-the-world which is quite different from a colleague who pilots his plane merely for the sake of making a living. Different matters will be significant for each pilot. Each pilot's understanding of himself or herself, and our understanding of each pilot, requires the disclosure of the Being-in-the-world of each pilot. We will thus learn the different way each pilot, as Dasein, exists its possibilities.

Heidegger states: "Dasein is the possibility of Being-free *for* its ownmost potentiality-for-Being."[2] He explains that Dasein's Being-there is essentially its understanding which discloses to itself what it is capable of. However, since Dasein's understanding is always accompanied by a mood, and since it lives its thrownness (a concept sketched below) without questioning it, it frequently fails to understand itself and to be free for its ownmost potentiality-for-being. Put differently, reaching true understanding of oneself as Being-there is no simple task. A major reason for the difficulties of attaining understanding is that Dasein always understands itself in terms of its possibilities, in terms of its being a project toward the future.

I wish to stress this major point. Heidegger holds that, for Dasein, understanding as a projection is primordial. Dasein's understanding includes a projection of its Being upon its for-the-sake-of-which, upon significance, and upon the worldhood of the world that it establishes. In short, Dasein is a thrown projection; thrown into its mood, and into the world that it helps to constitute, it projects this thrownness and its decisions upon the world.

Thus, Hamlet is thrown into a terrifying situation at the court in Elsinore, specifically when he meets the ghost of his father and learns that he was murdered by his uncle. This meeting throws Hamlet into a series of enigmatic moods that are unfathomable to Ophelia, to Polonius, to his mother, Gertrude, and to many others at the court. Hamlet projects upon the world his thrownness, and his not understanding himself, into this terrifying situation in which evil has triumphed. This projection of Hamlet's also reveals what is significant for him; he often describes his thoughts on this matter in soliloquies or in chance encounters with people. His projection is also expressed in Hamlet's procrastinations, his decisions, his play-acting, his understanding of the world, and finally, after reaching a resolution, his acts.

If, for the most part, Dasein understands itself in terms of its world, it is inauthentic. In contrast, authentic understanding arises out of Dasein's own self, through being wholly involved in its for-the-sake-of-which. Authentic understanding may lead to what Heidegger terms "sight," which is Dasein's access to entities and to Being. Dostoyevsky's Father Zosima in *The Brothers Karamazov*, mentioned in Chapter 1, attained such sight, which gave him access to perceiving the Being of many people whom he encountered. Such "sight," Heidegger adds, may come into being when Dasein is transparent to itself in relation to those matters which are central to its existence. Indeed, as Dostoyevski shows in detail, Zosima was transparent to himself.[3]

Knowledge can also lead Dasein to transparency and to "sight." This transparency must emerge in those realms which are constitutive for Dasein's existence, that is, its Being-alongside the world and its Being-with-Others. Such "sight," I would add to Heidegger's presentation, may lead to wisdom. In contrast, Dasein's opaqueness, which is quite common, is rooted in Dasein's self-deceptions and in its lack of acquaintance with the world.

* * *

Heidegger views interpretation as central to human existence: it emerges in all everyday matters. I almost never hear mere sounds, but rather, the rain pattering on the window or the siren of the police car. I almost never smell mere odors, but rather, the onions frying in the pan or the delicate fragrance of jasmine in the garden. I never taste sweetness, but rather, the thick, sticky sweetness of honey or the melting bitter-sweetness of a piece of bittersweet chocolate. Such is true for all senses. These immediate interpretations of what we encounter are almost always what constitute understanding. Through these immediate everyday interpretations, Dasein both projects its Being upon its possibilities and discovers itself in this projection and in these possibilities. Heidegger holds that through interpretation understanding becomes itself. Through immediately interpreting the soft drumming on the windowpane as the patter of rain, my understanding discloses possibilities for me and thus becomes itself.

Someone sensitive to the theme of this book may ask: Is the love of my beloved, which brings me joy and delight every day, merely an instance of my understanding? Is this love my mere interpretation of my beloved's smile, caress, and kiss? Furthermore, is my genuine comradeship with my friend Pierre, established years ago and tested over the years, solely an instance of my understanding and my interpretation? What are the ontological boundaries—if any—to interpretation? Is interpretation confined to those entities that are ready-to-hand and present-at-hand? Or does interpretation include the relations that come into being in Dasein's Being-with-Others and in its solicitude toward other Daseins?

In *Being and Time*, and in other texts from this period, Heidegger does not relate to these questions. Perhaps he ignored such questions because they bring up problems that are beyond his phenomenological approach and personal concern. I can say that he describes interpretation primarily as central to Dasein's relations to entities that are ready-to-hand and present-at hand.

In *Being and Time*, any interpretation is founded upon what Heidegger terms fore-having, fore-sight, and fore-conception. In my living room I have a windowpane (in advance of my interpreting the drumming on it). The windowpane is exposed to the elements of nature, which includes the changes of weather; such is fore-having. From my point of view as dweller in the house, the windowpane is necessary to allow light to penetrate the living room while keeping out the rain, the desert dust, the wind, and the excessive heat and cold. Consequently, I fore-see that a drumming upon the windowpane may be the patter of rain; such seeing in advance is fore-sight. However, to interpret the drumming on the pane as rain, I must beforehand be acquainted with certain concepts, such as "patter," "rain," and "window," that will allow me to determine what I am hearing. Thus, the articulated interpretation of the patter of rain emerges on the basis of a fore-conception. Based on this fore-having, fore-sight, and fore-conception, I can make the drumming I hear on the windowpane intelligible. I project meaning by determining, and interpreting, that the drumming that I hear is the patter of rain. Hence, meaning is an existentiale of Dasein, and fore-having, fore-sight, and fore-conception provide the structure for meaning.

Heidegger cautions the seeker for truth, advising him or her to refuse to accept uncritically those interpretations which are mere fancies and popular conceptions. Fore-having, fore-sight, and fore-conception assist in this task, since they are fore-structures which Dasein should work out in terms of the things that it encounters and the beings that exist. By a working out of the fore-structures of beings, Dasein can attain scientific knowledge. Indeed, scientific experiments, and much of scientific knowledge, are based on the working out of and attempting to determine the relationship between certain fore-structures and the things themselves. Of course, there is a circularity to this working out. Dasein's understanding becomes itself through interpretation. But Dasein's understanding also questions the validity of the fore-structures upon which any interpretation is based and changes them in accordance with the things themselves. This questioning and changing also leads to knowledge.

Heidegger presents no examples for the knowledge attained through the circular working out of the relation between the fore-structures and the things themselves. I would hold that the history of science provides some enlightening examples. Thus, the questioning of the then accepted fore-structures of cosmology by Copernicus, Galileo, and other thinkers, astronomers, and physicists of the fifteenth, sixteenth, and seventeenth centuries was a questioning which led to what we now term the Copernican revolution. This revolution is a remarkable example of attaining knowledge through the working out and the changing of the relation between fore-structures and the things themselves, which, in this case, were the stars and the planets.

* * *

A third existential element of Dasein's being "there," equiprimordial with its mood and its understanding, is discourse. Dasein's Being-in includes participating in discourse in which Dasein's Being-with is shared with other Daseins. Heidegger defines discourse as the articulation of intelligibility; it underlies interpretation and assertion. That which can be articulated in discourse, which gets expressed in language, he termed meaning. Thus, by participating in discourse, by putting matters of concern in words, Dasein can express the intelligibility of its Being-in-the-world. Discourse also discloses the concernful ways each Dasein maintains itself as Being-with other Daseins. In short, discourse helps to constitute Dasein's disclosing of its Being-in-the-world.

Four items are constitutive of discourse: what the discourse is about;

what is said-in-the-talk; the communication; and the making-known. Communication, which is the only one of the four that I shall discuss, means the articulation of Being with one another. Communication is what ensures that, through discourse, my Being-with another person becomes explicit: we share our Being-with each other. Someone might argue that communication might serve as the ground for love and friendship, but Heidegger gives no hints that such might be the case. The words *love* and *friendship* do not appear in this discussion—neither in his articulation of discourse nor in his description of communication. Furthermore, words such as *trust, dialogue*, and *responsibility*, which are central to genuine communication, and, of course, to love and friendship, are also lacking in his discussion of communication and Being-with. This lack, I would hold, is an unfortunate characteristic of Heidegger's fundamental ontology.

Let me explain. I believe that a major problem in the fundamental ontology that Heidegger presents is that genuine love and true friendship, trust, dialogue, and responsibility are not accounted for in his descriptions of discourse, communication, and the explicit sharing of Being-with. Again we should recall that descriptions and discussions of love and of friendship can be found in Plato's dialogues—which Heidegger studied diligently. In Plato's *Phaedrus*, for instance, Socrates reveals that true love is a wonderful, spiritually enhancing form of madness which may lead to wisdom. My personal experience, and also a host of literary and biographical examples, accord with many of Plato's ideas on love—as also with his descriptions of its blessings, as presented in *Phaedrus*. Yet almost no acknowledgment of Plato's ideas on the link between love and wisdom, as significant to Being-with and to communication between Daseins, can be found in Heidegger's writings of this period. Nor is such a discussion found in later writings. I can only conclude that Heidegger made no attempt to clarify the link between love, friendship, trust, dialogue, or responsibility and Dasein's Being-with. My reading reveals that his fundamental ontology has little place for these glorious moments of human existence.

* * *

Heidegger explains that it is not difficult to discern that, in its everyday thrownness, Dasein is often mastered by the "They." On the ontological level of Dasein's existence, this mastery by the "They" emerges in the phenomena of idle talk, curiosity, and ambiguity—which characterize the everyday being of Dasein. Heidegger stresses that he is not moralizing; he is merely presenting the ontological mastery of the "They" in Dasein's Being.

Idle talk constitutes the kind of being of Dasein's everyday interpreting and understanding. Spoken language is crucial for everyday understanding and interpreting. In spoken language, Dasein already encounters and is delivered to the specific understanding and interpretation of reality embraced by idle talk. Language already preserves what I would call the "chatter-inspired-understanding-interpretation" of the disclosed world and of other Daseins.

Thinking, therefore, requires that Dasein seek ways within language by which it may go beyond the everyday speaking and spokenness of language. Dasein must do so because, in this everyday language, the superficial understanding, presentation, and interpretation of reality, determined by idle talk, is ensconced. Such going beyond the everyday speaking and spokenness of language is very difficult, because idle talk and the interpretations stemming from idle talk are already established in Dasein's Being-in. Indeed, idle talk is established in Dasein's being, prior to its expressing a wish to think. Dasein can never totally extricate itself from the sodden bog of idle talk.

In order to think, in order to raise again the question of the meaning of Being, and also to distance himself from idle talk, Heidegger, like other great thinkers, coined many new terms. *Being-in-the-world* is one such term. Like other terms that he coined, and like the term *I–Thou* coined by Martin Buber, these new terms have been adopted by other philosophers and scholars. Heidegger's continual use of these terms in *Being and Time*, and in other writings, epitomizes his courageous striving to express his thinking in a language free of idle talk and its burden of shallowness.

Idle talk is shallow because in it there is no primary relationship to the Being of any entity discussed. Discourse characterized by idle talk does not appropriate an entity in a primordial manner; for instance, it does not relate to the essence of an entity, say, in the manner that Heidegger related to the essence of technology in his essay "The Question Concerning Technology."[4] Idle talk closes off realms of being and conceals entities in the world; it discourages inquiry and disputation on the Being of entities. Hence, idle talk communicates what it has to convey not by challenging or encouraging Dasein to think, but by gossip and by passing the word on. The result is very unfortunate. The average listener to and speaker of spoken language, in which the understanding and interpretation of idle talk prevail, and the average reader who is exposed to the widespread prevailing scribbling of chatter and gossip, which is written idle talk—such an average reader or listener develops and lives pretty much without thinking, and hence with a very shallow understanding of beings and of Being.

An outcome of the prevalence of idle talk in spoken language is that the "They" frequently prescribes Dasein's state of mind. In such a prescription, the "They" determines that Dasein should develop ungenuine relationships to beings, to other Daseins, to the world, and to Being.

Delivered to idle talk, Dasein's understanding is uprooted from the world of genuine relationships. In this situation, in which its understanding is constantly uprooted from genuine relationships, Dasein refrains from and rejects thinking. It floats, unattached and uncommitted, alongside beings and the world, supposedly communicating with other Daseins, but in truth merely waddling with them in the seepy bog of idle talk. In its uncommitted floating, Dasein is usually accompanied by many other Daseins who also float alongside beings and refrain from establishing genuine relations. Sheltered by idle talk from any questioning of their Being, and from raising the question of the meaning of Being, these Daseins drift together toward an ever-increasing groundlessness in their existence. Such a continual uprooting of its Being and its understanding, accompanied by directionless floating alongside beings, is Dasein's everyday reality. Heidegger adds with insight that it is a most stubborn reality.

* * *

Curiosity, according to Heidegger, concerns itself with seeing, not in order to reach an understanding or to obtain knowledge of what is seen, but merely so as to see something. It is a search for novelty, in order to jump immediately to a new novelty. Heidegger's presentation of curiosity can be contrasted with his views on wonder. He often mentions Socrates' saying in Plato's dialogue *Theaetetus*: "wonder is the feeling of the philosopher, and philosophy begins in wonder."[5]

When I wonder, I often endeavor to discern what arouses my wonder with greater clarity. I may frequently strive to attain more knowledge and understanding of that which arouses my wonder. Wonder may lead to an examination of beings in the world, to a search for knowledge of the essence of a being, to the pursuit of wisdom, and, perhaps, even to addressing the question of the meaning of Being. No such search for worthy knowledge or wisdom characterizes curiosity, or accompanies curiosity. It is a kind of knowing, but only in order to have known. Thus, many people are very curious about the love life of some major political figures; satisfying such curiosity, as many popular books and newspapers do, very rarely leads to worthy knowledge.

Heidegger describes three major characteristics of curiosity: not tarrying in the environment in which it expressed concern; being constantly distracted by new items; never dwelling anywhere. By never dwelling anywhere he means that Dasein's curiosity is everywhere and nowhere, skipping from topic to topic, never attempting to find a ground for the paltry and novel knowledge that it obtains. Consequently, blended with idle talk, curiosity adds to the uprooting of Dasein. How does this blend occur?

Idle talk dictates what Dasein must know in order to be what is today termed "in," which means knowing what today concerns the "They." One can only be "in," however, by constantly jumping from novelty to novelty, that is, by being constantly curious. But since the Being of curiosity is everywhere and nowhere, such a being can be articulated only by idle talk, by understanding and interpretation that seek no worthy knowledge of the essence of beings. Hence, it is not difficult to describe the vicious circle: the uprootedness of idle talk from the Being of beings drags Dasein to embrace curiosity and to constantly seek novelties; and the uprootedness of curiosity, which is also groundless, drags Dasein to constantly engage in idle talk.

When the "They" masters Dasein's existence, ambiguity is common. A person whose discourse is flooded with ambiguity is fleeing from responsibility. Furthermore, ambiguity is linked to the essential groundlessness of idle talk and curiosity. Due to this groundlessness the understanding of the "They" brings no true knowledge, and any view is acceptable, including blatantly ambiguous views. When Dasein is totally delivered to the "They" and to its groundless understanding and interpretation, it finds it almost impossible to distinguish between genuine knowledge and falsities and fakes. The result is an ambiguity in Dasein's Being and in its Being-with Others. Dasein acts as if everything were genuinely understood, genuinely grasped, genuinely spoken, though it is not thus. The opposite is also possible: matters do not look as if they were genuinely grasped, understood, and spoken, but they are.

Heidegger gives no examples of ambiguity, but one can easily perceive that probably most politicians speak and act ambiguously. Their followers and many of their faithful listeners, however, flee from recognizing this easily discernable ambiguity. They choose to believe that the matter at hand is genuinely spoken, hence merely needs to be genuinely grasped and genuinely understood.

A fine literary example of such ambiguity is presented in William Shakespeare's play *Julius Caesar*. Mark Antony presents a demagogic speech to the Romans, shortly after Caesar was murdered by Brutus and his fellow conspirators. The Romans refuse to perceive the ambiguity in Antony's speech, an ambiguity that members of the audience in the theater grasp immediately (act 3, scene 2). These Romans grasp Antony's speech as genuinely spoken and themselves as genuinely grasping and genuinely understanding what has happened. In truth, Shakespeare shows, they grasp and understand nothing; their stupidity helps the wickedness of Antony and Octavius to triumph. Unfortunately, even today, it is still very common for many people to embrace and to supposedly genuinely grasp the ambiguity of a wily politician's speeches as genuinely spoken words.

Ambiguity is central to the discourse of the "They," to idle talk, and curiosity. Much too often, when Dasein flees responsibility and commitment or genuine knowledge and understanding, it does so by engaging in idle talk or by bringing up matters that will arouse curiosity. Through such responses Dasein resists all attempts to efface the ambiguity embedded in its existence.

In Leo Tolstoy's *Anna Karenina*, you will find a poignant description of one such person who refuses to acknowledge the ambiguity of his existence. I am referring to Marshal Sviazhsky, whom Levin, a major figure in the novel, visits.

Sviazhsky was one of those people who always amazed Levin because their extremely logical, though never original ideas were kept in a watertight compartment and had no influence whatever on their extremely definite and stable lives, which went on quite independently and almost diametrically opposed to them. Sviazhsky was an extremely liberal person. He despised the nobility and considered the majority of noblemen to be secretly in favor of serfdom, though too cowardly to express their views openly. He considered Russia to be a doomed country, like Turkey, and the Russian government so bad that he did not think it worth his while to criticize its actions; yet he was a civil servant, a model marshal of the nobility, and when he traveled he always wore a peaked cap with a red band and a cockade.[6]

Tolstoy continues to describe in detail the contradictions and the ambiguity in Sviazhsky's discourse and everyday existence. Heidegger's terms help to define Sviazhsky's Dasein. He is uprooted, lives a life dictated by the "They," and is steeped in ambiguity. He, seemingly, does not recognize the ambiguity that is central to his being. Sviazhsky's not recognizing the core of ambiguity in his existence accords with Heidegger's thinking—he already lives with ambiguity as supposedly natural to his language, discourse, and life. Tolstoy, however, goes one step further, which is important for the theme of my inquiry. He describes Levin's continual failures in his attempts to reach authentic dialogue with Sviazhsky. As far as I know, Heidegger never clearly stated a major insight that repeatedly appears in Tolstoy's novels: by engaging in genuine dialogue, one can, at times, free oneself from the mastery of the "They," with its idle talk, curiosity, and ambiguity.

Heidegger uses the term *fallenness* to denote Dasein's being absorbed in the publicness of the "They," the publicness which has been established by other Daseins who are constantly guided by idle talk, curiosity, and ambiguity. By "fallenness" he means that Dasein has fallen away from its authentic potentiality for being its self; it falls into inauthenticity and into being lost in the "They." In vivid poetic terms, Heidegger states that Dasein is sucked into the turbulence of the "They's" inauthenticity. He indicates that for the most part Dasein maintains itself as fallen and inauthentic, while being fascinated by the world, and by its Dasein-with other fallen inauthentic Daseins.

The term *fallenness* also points to Dasein's temptation to fall into a tranquilizing inauthenticity. Dasein attains "fallenness" by existing solely in the realm of idle talk, which accepts and promotes the superficial way all matters of concern have been interpreted by the public. Yielding to the temptation of fallenness, as many Daseins do, means losing oneself in the "They," falling into groundlessness, embracing inauthenticity, and living a drifting alienated existence. Heidegger adds that in contemporary life, this alienation is often accompanied by a (psychological) self-dissection which usually leads nowhere, except to self-entanglement—never to authenticity.

* * *

The presentation of Dasein's Being-in completes the phenomenological elucidation of the constitutive items of Being-in-the-world. Yet Dasein, as a whole, transcends its constituting items. Heidegger asks, How can Dasein as a structural whole be defined in an existential ontological manner?

He reiterates that Dasein has a kind of Being that becomes disclosed to itself as thrown into the world. As such, Dasein is its possibilities, it understands itself in terms of and through these possibilities, and it projects itself upon these possibilities. Usually, however, Dasein exists its thrownness inauthentically, as a "They"-self. Consequently, to comprehend Dasein as a structural whole, and as authentic, we must seek a state of mind and understanding in which the totality of Dasein is disclosed to itself, severed from the "They."

Such a state of mind is anxiety. Heidegger holds that anxiety can provide the phenomenal basis for grasping Dasein's primordial totality and for its revealing itself as care. With the understanding of Dasein's structural whole as care, the question of the meaning of Being can again be raised. But raising this question requires clarifying the link between Being and truth, which have been connected, Heidegger states, since time immemorial. Thus, understanding anxiety, as a distinctive way in which Dasein is disclosed, is the first step in his presentation of authentic Dasein.

While briefly indicating Heidegger's path of thinking concerning anxiety and Dasein's totality, I suggest that three questions which are relevant to the theme of this book be kept in mind: (1) Are there not other states of mind, such as joy or genuine love, in which the totality of Dasein is disclosed to itself? (2) Cannot joy and love also provide the phenomenal basis for grasping Dasein's primordial totality? (3) In choosing to discuss anxiety, has not Heidegger chosen a particularly lonely state of mind, when compared to joy or genuine love?

As we learned from Kierkegaard, anxiety is not fear. I fear a specific entity in the world. But Dasein is anxious not about a specific entity; it is anxious in face of its Being-in-the-world and in face of its primordial homelessness in the world. In order to soothe its anxiety, and to tranquilize itself in face of its homelessness in the world, very often Dasein flees itself and its authenticity into being absorbed in the "They." If anxiety is not soothed, if anxiety is faced courageously, it can lead, Heidegger holds, to a worthier existence. By bringing Dasein to face its Being-in-the-world, by bringing it to see its flight from itself, by making manifest to Dasein its being "not-at-home" in the world as primordial to its existence, anxiety discloses to Dasein its Being—free to choose itself and its ownmost potentiality for Being. Hence, anxiety may bring Dasein face to face with what Heidegger calls its Being-free for the authenticity of its Being. Indeed, by facing anxiety, Dasein may reach worthy decisions, which may lead it to live a worthy life and to exist authentically.

Dasein's anxiety, Dasein's Being-free for its ownmost potentiality-for-Being, characterize it as an entity whose Being is an issue. In a rather circular manner we can state that the issue is how a specific Dasein will respond to anxiety and to its Being-free for its ownmost potentiality-for-Being. Thus, to refer once more to the above example, Hamlet at first flees anxiety into procrastinations and into playacting an assumed madness. When he begins to face his anxiety straightforwardly, Hamlet senses that he is free to fulfill his ownmost potentiality-for-Being. In Chapter 3, I bring a soliloquy by Hamlet that vividly reveals the change he undergoes when he decides to face his anxiety straightforwardly.

Dasein's Being-free for its ownmost potentiality-for-Being means that, as Being in the world, Dasein is also in the state of Being ahead of itself. The totality of Dasein is expressed in its Being-ahead-of-itself-in-the-world, which means that Dasein is always concerned with the future and with the world. In a word, Dasein is absorbed in the world of its concern. This concern, this Being-ahead-of-itself, relates to the facticity of the world, to the future of Dasein, and to its choice of its unique for-the-sake-of-which.

Using these locutions, Heidegger defines a term that is central to his ontology: care. *Care* summarizes for Heidegger, in a single short word, the fact that, primodially, Dasein is a Being that exists both ahead-of-itself-Being-already-in-the-world and as Being-alongside the entities that it encounters in the world. Here *care* is an ontological term; it is an abbreviated manner of expressing the complexity of the primordial structure of Dasein's Being-in-the-world. It precedes an anthropology of Dasein and also precedes concrete acts such as that of willing or deciding. Concern with entities ready-to-hand, and solicitude toward other Daseins, are both based on care.

As Heidegger defines care, however, it is not linked in any direct man-

ner to responsibility—neither responsibility for other persons nor responsibility for the fate of the world. In this context, concern and
solicitude have no moral links or implications. Someone may suggest
that the term "Being-free for one's ownmost potentiality-for-Being" already includes responsibility—but Heidegger never makes such a statement. Furthermore, at best, "Being-free for one's ownmost potentiality
for Being" seems to relate to responsibility for oneself, not to responsibility for others or for the fate of the world. I would add that the term
responsibility appears rarely in Heidegger's writings on ontology and on
other topics.[7]

Here some questions emerge. Despite the flexibility of language, by
using the term *care* in a manner that totally divorces it from responsibility, is not Heidegger distorting the term? Does not this use of *care* also
distort the ontology of Dasein? Indeed, is it ontologically correct to describe Dasein's Being as a Being-in-the-world that, seemingly, has min-
imal responsibility toward other Daseins, and almost no responsibility
for the fate of the world that it shares with others?

Further questions arise, but first, once again consider Plato, whose
ontology was developed in detail in his dialogue *The Republic*, which
deals with justice. It is also worthy of mention that Heidegger repeatedly
refers to Plato and that he chose a citation from Plato as the motto of
Being and Time. Does it, therefore, not seem strange that Heidegger ignores, and to the best of my knowledge never mentions, Plato's insight
that a true ontology of humans must be linked to the pursuit of the Good
and to the search for justice? Did not Heidegger make a grave mistake
when he did not relate, in his discussion of care, to Plato's linking of
ontology to justice?

I can only conclude that the term *care* as Heidegger redefines it may
provide some ontological insights. However, it is also a rather castrated
term when compared to the use of the term in human discourse. Furthermore, the castration of this term, *care*, seems to reveal a major lacuna
in relation to human responsibility and to justice in Heidegger's ontology. I return to this topic later.

* * *

Heidegger cites an ancient Latin fable in which Dasein is interpreted
as care, and care is considered to be ontologically prior to all other com-
portments of Dasein. He believes that this fable helps him to justify his
interpretation of Being-in-the-world as care. In subsequent chapters of
Being and Time, he will show that care is ontologically prior through its
links to time. At this point, he returns to the question of the meaning of
Being, and, on the basis of his path of thinking, attempts to reach a better
understanding of Being. Such is hindered, he complains, by the accepted
situation wherein Being has acquired the meaning of Reality and sub-

stantiality has become the basic characteristic of Being. Put differently, for many thinkers and laypeople, Being has been diverted to mean Reality which is considered to be some sort of complex substance. To counter this state of affairs, Heidegger first examines what he calls "the problem of Reality."

Many thinkers linked Reality to the question of whether the external world can be proved by the consciousness that beholds it. Heidegger holds that the existential analytic which he presented has eliminated such questioning. According to this existential analytic, access to entities within-the-world, which constitute the Real, is through knowing and is founded upon Dasein's Being-in-the-world; but for Dasein, care, as its state of Being, is even more primordial. Such an ontology reveals that the question of whether there is an external world makes no sense. Of course, Dasein as Being-in-the-world may raise the question of what is Real, but the world is disclosed together with the Being of Dasein. Thus, the scandal of philosophy is that proofs of the external world are repeatedly attempted and presented—without providing any ontological basis. These so-called proofs assume a subject which is worldless, an assumption which is foolish, at best.

Someone may still ask, Does the term *Reality* contribute any additional insights to Heidegger's existential analytic?—Not at all. After describing certain flawed attempts to relate to the Being of Reality, Heidegger states that the terms *Reality* and *substantiality* have nothing to contribute to our understanding of entities with Dasein's kind of Being.

Heidegger next questions the assumption that the essence of truth is in the agreement of a judgment with its object. According to this assumption, my judgment "That tree is an oak" will be true if the tree to which I am referring is indeed an oak tree. Heidegger holds, however, that such an agreeing can only emerge if there exists a Being that uncovers certain entities and discloses their manner of Being. This disclosing Being is Dasein, who can state that an assertion is true when it uncovers an entity as what it is. Moreover: "Uncovering is a way of Being for Being-in-the-world."[8]

Thus, truths about entities in the world can be uncovered only to a Being who exists as Being-in-the-world and whose way of Being is to uncover. Heidegger states categorically that the state of Being of Dasein which he calls disclosedness is the foundation for the primordial phenomenon of truth. This primordial truth he calls, using the Greek name, *aletheia*, which means the unconcealed. Dasein brings forth truth, aletheia, from concealment. Heidegger adds that only a Being who exists as disclosedness can uncover the tree as an oak; and only after the initial unconcealment, the uncovering, can Dasein make judgments pertaining to that tree.

Heidegger here formulates a major principle: "Dasein is in the truth."[9]

He clarifies this principle with four considerations already elucidated. First, disclosedness, and hence truth, essentially belongs to Dasein's state of Being. Being-in-the-world, or care, means disclosing entities in the world. Second, Dasein is thrown into a definite world in which definite entities factually exist which can be disclosed. Third, since Dasein is a potentiality-for-Being, to which disclosedness belongs as a state of Being, Dasein can attain the most authentic disclosedness, which is truth as existence. Fourth, because Dasein's state of Being is very often falling, because it is usually governed by the "They" with its idle talk, curiosity, and ambiguity, most entities that Dasein encounters are not uncovered in their true Being. In its state of falling, Dasein is in untruth. Governed by the "They," fallen Dasein is in a realm characterized by untruth, that is, by undisclosedness of entities, of itself, and of Being.

Heidegger explains: Only because Dasein is in truth can it be in untruth; only because disclosedness belongs to Dasein as a state of Being it is possible to cover up entities, or not disclose them, or to disguise them. Hence, Dasein is equiprimordially both in truth and in untruth. Yet, since Dasein is in the truth, it is essential for Dasein's Being to pursue truth, to appropriate what has been uncovered and to reject all semblance and anything counterfeit. The uncovering of truth is always on the basis of semblance, in which something is partially uncovered, or hints at what may be uncovered and disclosed. Heidegger adds: Dasein must often snatch entities out of their hiddenness so as to disclose truth; the factical uncovering of beings is often a kind of robbery.

If truth is based on Dasein's disclosedness, if truth belongs to the basic constitution of Dasein, why is truth usually described as the agreement of an assertion with facts? The ontological reason emerges when we recognize that Dasein expresses itself as a Being-toward entities; indeed, Dasein is a Being-toward entities to whom discourse belongs. Dasein expresses itself in language as an uncoverer of entities. Often an assertion is an expression of Dasein's uncovering of certain entities; it is the communicating of what this uncovering of entities discloses to other Daseins. Even when I convey an assertion which has been affirmed by another person, say, that Sequoia trees grow in California, or that Hesiod's poetry deals with justice, the assertion retains its being 's an uncovering, as a disclosedness of certain entities. As such, the assertion itself becomes an entity that is ready-to-hand, but it remains grounded in Dasein's disclosedness.

Truth, Heidegger holds, is an existentiale. A major consequence of this determination is: Since Dasein brings truth into being, truth will exist only as long as there are Daseins who will uncover truths and convey them to each other. Before Isaac Newton, the truths that he discovered concerning, say, the force of gravity or the spectrum of light were neither true nor false—they were simply not yet disclosed, or, if you wish, still covered. Consequently, Heidegger states, we cannot speak of eternal truths until we can prove that Dasein will exist for all eternity—which is quite dubious. However, the fact that Dasein discloses truths does not mean that truth is subjective, in the sense that each person can claim his or her own truth. Truth is subjective only in the sense that Dasein as Being-in-the-world, and as care, uncovers specific entities and frees them for itself and for other Daseins. Certain Daseins may formulate assertions which relate to these uncovered, freed entities. For instance, I can affirm or reject specific characteristics of this Sequoia tree.

Although Heidegger's insights concerning truth are very enlightening, the same problem that I already mentioned also emerges here. He does not mention a crucial area of human existence in which truth may emerge. Language discloses this area in simple statements such as: Joseph is a true friend; Sarah experienced true love. In these statements, it is not certain entities that are ready-to-hand or present-at-hand that are uncovered or disclosed. Rather, certain specific relations between two persons are described as true. Let me say it again. Friendship and love cannot be described as entities; consequently, these relations cannot be viewed as ready-to-hand or present-at-hand. True friendship and true love come into being in a mysterious way between two particular persons. What is more, these relations exist only as long as both persons direct their whole being toward each other, as partners in the living event of friendship and love.

Using some of Heidegger's basic insights, I would add a most significant point concerning human relations. When, say, between Jacob and Rachel a true love comes into being and flourishes, a wonderful and blessed dimension of human existence, a dimension that is frequently covered and hidden, has been uncovered and disclosed. However, in developing his fundamental ontology, and in presenting his existential analytic of Dasein, Heidegger never related to the coming into being or the Being of true love—nor of true friendship. Consequently, we should not wonder that he rejected the I–Thou.

NOTES

1. Søren Kierkegaard, *The Concept of Anxiety*, trans. Reidar Thomte with Albert B. Anderson (Princeton, NJ: Princeton University Press, 1980), p. 42.

2. Martin Heidegger, *Being and Time*, trans. John Macquarrie and Edward Robinson (Oxford, Eng.: Basil Blackwell, 1962), p. 182.

3. Fyodor Dostoyevsky, *The Brothers Karamazov*, trans. Richard Pevear and Larissa Volokhonsky (New York: Vintage, 1991). See especially book 6, "The Russian Monk."

4. Martin Heidegger, *The Question Concerning Technology and Other Essays*, trans. William Lovitt (New York: Harper & Row, 1977).

5. Plato, *Theaetetus The Collected Dialogues*, ed. Edith Hamilton and Huntington Cairns (Princeton, N.J.: Princeton University Press, 1961), [155].

6. Leo Tolstoy, *Anna Karenina*, trans. David Magarshack (New York: New American Library, 1961), p. 334.

7. Consider Martin Heidegger, *The Basic Problems of Phenomenology*, trans. Albert Hofstadter (Bloomington: Indiana University Press, 1982). This book is discussed in Chapters 4 and 5. A few times in the book responsibility is mentioned, for instance: "To the complete concept of personalitas belongs not only rationality but also responsibility" (p. 132). However, Heidegger here is explaining Kant's views, not his own.

8. Heidegger, *Being and Time*, p. 263.

9. Ibid.

Chapter 3

Dasein and Temporality

Central to the fundamental ontology that Heidegger presents in *Being and Time* is the linking of Dasein's possibility of Being-a-whole to its Being-toward-death and to temporality. This linking is Heidegger's manner of coping with the profound difficulties inherent in trying to grasp Dasein's Being-a-whole.

One prominent difficulty is that Dasein, as care, is always primarily ahead-of-itself, which means that Dasein exists for the sake of itself. Put otherwise, since Dasein is defined as a being whose existence is always directed ahead-of-itself, Dasein is concentrated primarily, and often solely, in its future being; therefore it exists for the sake of itself. This conclusion emerges because care is defined in a manner that gives a diminished role to other persons in the basic constitution of Dasein. However, at least theoretically, someone could suggest that Dasein, as care, may be defined as ahead-of-itself-and-of-other-persons. It seems that Heidegger never considered this possibility.

The term *ahead-of-itself* indicates that, in the basic constitution of Dasein, there is always something outstanding; there is always something not fulfilled in Dasein's potentiality-for-Being, something which has not become actual. Put differently, when Dasein reaches the stage that absolutely nothing more is still outstanding for it, it *is there* no longer as Dasein. At that moment Dasein has ceased to exist as a Being-in-the-world. A corpse remains, not a living human being. Thus, Heidegger asserts, Dasein's basic constitution is such that it never attains wholeness. Yet, he asks, is it impossible to grasp the wholeness of Dasein? Can we find a way to make this wholeness accessible? In seeking an answer to these questions, he examines Dasein's relationship to death.

When Dasein, supposedly, attains wholeness by perishing, it is no longer Dasein. Consequently, Dasein cannot describe the experience of perishing from the personal perspective of one who has fully experienced it and perished. Dasein's not being able to experience death and remain Dasein leads it to be impressed by the death of Others, where it meets death outside itself, seemingly as something objective. In the death of the Other, Dasein encounters a Being-in-the-world that, by perishing, has become something present-at-hand. A Dasein has become a no-longer-Dasein; it has become a corpse.

The deceased Dasein has abandoned the world which it established together with other Daseins, and the Daseins who remain may experience the loss. But this experience of loss has no link to the loss-of-Being which the Dasein who perished suffered. This loss of Being cannot be grasped by Dasein. At most, Dasein can undergo the experience of being alongside a person who is dying. But this being alongside only brings Dasein to witness death as experienced by the Other; it does not bring Dasein face to face with its own death.

Thus, comprehending the perishing of others cannot be a substitute for an ontological analysis of Dasein's totality and wholeness. This ontological analysis commences with the perception that dying is a very personal matter. Every Dasein must, when the time comes, take upon itself its own dying. No one can take away from any Dasein its own dying. In this sense, dying is constitutive for Dasein's wholeness. But since no experience of its own dying is available to Dasein, its totality still eludes our comprehension and analysis.

After considering some conceptual difficulties, Heidegger proffers an existential-ontological sketch of the structure of death. He presents death from a phenomenological perspective. For Dasein, death is distinctively impending, since it is not something that Dasein can experience and remain Dasein. It is nonrelational, since with a person's death all relations with other Daseins have ended. Death is Dasein's ownmost possibility, which it cannot outstrip. It is the possibility of no longer being Dasein, of no longer Being-in-the-world, of becoming a corpse. Because Dasein is a being that is disclosed to itself as ahead-of-itself, Dasein knows that it will die. Heidegger believes that Dasein's being ahead-of-itself, which is central to the structure of care, "has its most primordial concretion in Being-toward-death."[1]

Heidegger explains: As a result of its existing, Dasein has been thrown into a world in which it faces its death as its ownmost possibility, which is not outstripped and is nonrelational. Put differently, Dasein knows that the basic situation of Being-in-the-world includes Dasein's being delivered over to its own death. In moments of anxiety, Dasein may comprehend and suffer acutely from its being thrown into the world and from facing death as its ownmost possibility. It may sink into anxiety when comprehending the possibility of its death. Very often, Dasein flees anxiety and this possibility of facing its own death. Dasein covers up its Being-toward-death by falling into and involving itself in everyday concerns. But this flight, this embracing of inauthenticity, can never efface the fact: for Dasein, dying is grounded in Being-in-the-world, and in care.

The link between Being-toward-death and care emerges in the everydayness of Dasein. Since the "They" determines the inauthentic self of everydayness, Dasein expresses and interprets its everyday self, and especially its Being-toward-death, by engaging in idle talk, supported by curiosity and ambiguity. According to the understanding and interpretation of the "They," death is an objective event that is continually ocurring in the world, an event best relegated to inconspicuousness. The "They" speaks of death in an alienated, distanced, ambiguous manner: someday one will die. My own death is not yet present-at-hand, hence it is not a threat. In short, death as my ownmost possibility is leveled down by the "They." Through this leveling down, my impending death becomes an event that belongs to nobody, and definitely not to myself. The "They" perverts death, which is my ownmost possibility, into a public occurrence, a case, a happening.

When in everyday life Dasein's own death is persistently covered up, Dasein no longer relates to its ownmost potentiality-for-Being. Dasein has lost its self in the "They," which offers it a constant tranquilization about death. Immersed in this indifferent and inauthentic tranquility, Dasein may often consider the dying of the Other to be a social inconvenience, a nuisance, a tactlessness of the person who is dying, against which the public should be guarded. Together with the inauthentic tranquility that it promotes and imposes, the "They" tacitly regulates how Dasein should comport itself toward death. The "They" not only establishes funeral institutions, rites, and customs. Much more important, the "They" strives to eradicate the likelihood that Dasein courageously, with anxiety, will face its own death as a possibility which is not to be outstripped. In addition, the "They" endeavors to transform anxiety in the face of death into fear about future events, for instance, the fear of suffering before death. Such fear is derided as a weakness, since it interferes with the indifferent tranquility in the face of death that the "They" persistently cultivates. It should be evident, however, that the cultivation of this indifference alienates Dasein from its potentiality-for-Being and from its freedom.

Alienated, indifferent, and tranquilized, Dasein's everyday kind of Being is a "falling," which is a persistent flight from facing its own death. When confronted by the fact of death, Dasein concedes that certainly everyone will die; but it relates to this certainty in an ambiguous manner, not as its own distinctive possibility. Consequently, in most cases, Dasein's "falling" is inauthentic and an evasion of its Being-toward-death. This evasion leads Dasein to exist in untruth.

As I have shown, Heidegger holds that truth emerges when Dasein uncovers and discloses a being or an aspect of Being. Recall again, the Greek term that Heidegger uses for truth, *aletheia*, which means unconcealed. Hence, when in everyday existence Dasein persistently covers up its ownmost possibility, when it veils from itself its own death, when it relentlessly flees the anxiety of facing its own death, when it does its utmost so that its own death will not be unconcealed, Dasein exists in untruth. Without presenting additional aspects of Heidegger's detailed description of Dasein's inauthentic relation to death, the question arises: Can Dasein understand and relate authentically to its ownmost possibility, to its death?

* * *

Heidegger explains that in order to relate to its own death authentically, Dasein must accept its death as a distinctive possibility of its Being. Death is not a possibility that is ready-to-hand or present-at-hand, but a possibility of Dasein's existence. Moreover, death differs from other possibilities that Dasein faces because, in Dasein's life, death "is to show as little as possible of its possibility."[2] Dasein does not expect death as it expects other possibilities, for which it waits to be actualized. Put differently, Dasein may anticipate its death, as the possibility of the impossibility of its existence; but Dasein does not expect its own death, as, say, I expect a close friend to come by for dinner.

For Dasein, anticipating and understanding the possibility of its death means grasping death as the impossibility of any existence at all. Dasein cannot picture this impossibility to itself, nor can it find ways to measure it so as to make it more comprehensible. However, Dasein can relate its anticipation of its own death, in which its very Being is at issue, to its potentiality-for-being. An existence in which such a relating emerges is authentic. Hence, existing authentically is often fraught with anxiety. For this authentic existence to become a possibility, Dasein must, in Heidegger's terms, wrench itself away from the "They." When such a wrenching away from the "They" succeeds, Dasein's anticipation of its death means that it has become free to comprehend a sad truth: death lays claim to it as an individual. In a word, death individualizes Dasein.

Someone may ask: Why should I put emphasis on anticipation of my death as individualizing my being? Is it not possible that relations such as true love or genuine friendship may lay claim to an individual Dasein? Can we not state that a way of life dedicated to the search for wisdom— think of Socrates—may lay claim to a person? Furthermore, is it not true that the struggle for justice—Mahatma Gandhi's and Nelson Mandela's struggles for justice again come to mind—may lay claim to an individual Dasein?

Heidegger's answer is that death as Dasein's ownmost possibility is nonrelational; as such it individualizes Dasein fully and profoundly. This answer rings true, but I doubt that it is the entire truth. The questions in the preceding paragraph also pose authentic and truthful ways in which human existence can be individualized.

Heidegger, however, holds that Dasein's anticipation of its death is primal for authentically being alongside the world or for engaging in any authentic relation with other Daseins. Put differently, only if Dasein authentically anticipates its ownmost possibility, its death, can Dasein authentically be concerned with other beings in the world or engage in solicitude toward other Daseins. In addition, he suggests, anticipation of its own death may endow Dasein with an understanding of the potentiality-for-Being of other Daseins. One consequence of this answer is that in order to establish worthy relations with others, such as relations of concern or solicitude, Dasein must first become an individual by authentically anticipating its own death. It is not clear why Heidegger does not develop this theme.

Anticipation of its own death, which means being free for its own death, often liberates Dasein from being lost in those possibilities which are thrust upon it by some difficult or frustrating accident of life. As already suggested, such an anticipation is often accompanied by anxiety. Heidegger does not state so, but he indicates that freedom towards death may lead to a conversion in which a person chooses to act and live differently. For such a conversion to come into being, in which a new genuine freedom emerges, in which a person decides to live resolutely in anticipation of his or her own death, the person must abandon many of the illusions of the "They." He or she must courageously live with anxiety, and with the constant threat of being thrown "there" into a specific, often difficult, situation. Such a person must also courageously face the specific adverse facts which currently constitute his or her Being-in-the-world and the certainty of his or her own death.

I have already briefly indicated in Chapter 2 that Hamlet's life and plight accord with some of Heidegger's insights concerning human existence. I believe that a rather lengthy soliloquy by Hamlet will help to partially illuminate the thoughts of Heidegger on Dasein's resolutely facing its own death. In this example, by resolutely facing his own death, Hamlet begins to liberate himself from being entangled and enmeshed in those difficult possibilities which were thrust upon him by the vile crimes that he discovered in the court at Elsinore. The example of Hamlet's existential situation, during this moment of soliloquy, will also make intelligible additional insights that are proffered by Heidegger—insights that are discussed later in this chapter.

The moment that Hamlet chooses for his liberating soliloquy is significant. Hamlet meets the army of Fortinbras marching through Denmark, on their way to fight for what they recognize to be a worthless plot of Polish land. Immediately after encountering an officer of Fortinbras's army, who describes their marching to war so as "to gain a little patch of ground That hath in it no profit but the name," Hamlet seems to undergo a conversion (act 4, scene 4). He recognizes and rejects the many procrastinations and the persistent playacting that until now characterized his existence. He seems to anticipate the possibility of his own death and the need to face it resolutely. Here is his painful, yet enlightening, soliloquy:

> How all occasions do inform against me,
> And spur my dull revenge! What is a man,
> If his chief good and market of his time
> Be but to sleep and feed? a beast, no more.
> Sure he that made us with such large discourse,
> Looking before and after, gave us not
> That capability and godlike reason
> To fust in us unus'd. Now, whether it be
> Bestial oblivion or some craven scruple
> Of thinking too precisely on the event,—
> A thought which, quarter'd, hath but one part wisdom
> And ever three parts coward,—I do not know
> Why yet I live to say, "This thing's to do,"
> Sith I have cause, and will, and strength, and means
> To do't. Examples, gross as earth, exhort me:
> Witness this army, of such mass and charge,
> Led by a delicate and tender prince,
> Whose spirit, with divine ambition puff'd,
> Making mouths at the invisible event;
> Exposing what is mortal and unsure
> To all that fortune, death, and danger dare,
> Even for an egg-shell. Rightly to be great
> Is not to stir without great argument,
> But greatly to find quarrel in a straw
> When honour's at the stake. How stand I,
> That have a father kill'd, a mother stain'd
> Excitements of my reason and my blood,
> And let all sleep? while, to my shame, I see
> The imminent death of twenty thousand men,
> That, for a fantasy and trick of fame,
> Go to their graves like beds; fight for a plot
> Whereon the numbers cannot try the cause,
> Which is not tomb enough and continent
> To hide the slain?—O, from this time forth,
> My thoughts be bloody, or be nothing worth! (act 4, scene 4)

As indicated, Hamlet's statements reveal that he is beginning to free himself from being entangled and enmeshed in the difficult possibilities thrust upon him after he learned that his uncle murdered his father and wedded his mother. He now perceives the banality in his "thinking too precisely on the event,—/A thought which, quartered, hath but one part wisdom/And ever three parts coward." Yet, knowing that in his own Being thoughts should lead to deeds, Hamlet concludes his conversion with the moving statement: "O, from this time forth,/My thoughts be bloody, or be nothing worth!"

Need I add that in the soliloquy Hamlet seems to have decided to face his own death resolutely, and hence to act authentically? Shakespeare's text seems to accord with such an understanding of Hamlet's conversion. After Hamlet acknowledges, in the soliloquy, his own cowardice, and after his firm rejection of mere playing with thoughts, in the following scenes of the tragedy, Hamlet acts authentically and courageously against the evil surrounding him.

* * *

Hamlet's soliloquy also has implications for what Heidegger terms Dasein's response to a call of conscience. When Dasein is lost in the "They" self, it is characterized by its *not* choosing its possibilities. The "They" even conceals the fact that it has relieved Dasein of choosing its possibilities. In such a situation, Dasein continually "gets carried along by the nobody."[3] To emerge from inauthentic existence, from its own inauthentic Self, Dasein must choose to make a choice that will bring forth its potentiality-for-Being. Through such a decision to choose, Dasein may begin to find its true Self.

Heidegger explains: Dasein already is a potentiality-for-Being-its-Self, but this potentiality has to be attested. In everyday existence this potentiality is attested by Dasein's "voice of conscience," which is not something present at hand. Viewed ontologically, conscience is a call, it is an appeal to Dasein to live its ownmost potentiality-for-Being-its-Self. However, since Dasein usually evades such an existence, the call of conscience summons it to face its Being-guilty.

The call of conscience is an appeal to Dasein's understanding, which together with disclosedness and mood, constitute its Being-there. To respond to this appeal, Dasein must first hear it. When Dasein is lost in the "They," however, it fails to hear itself and listens only to the "They." Among the reasons for its failure is that the call of conscience requires another kind of hearing, a hearing which is essentially different from the listening that Dasein adopts when it is lost in the "They." The call of conscience is an understanding that rejects and transcends the idle talk, the ambiguity, and the curiosity that characterize the discourse of the "They." Only when a firm and authentic rejecting and transcending of the "They" occurs will Dasein hear the call of conscience and understand it as a summons into its ownmost potentiality-for-Being-its-Self.

Hamlet's anguish, as expressed in his soliloquy, cited above, in which he recognizes his previous cowardice, seems to be the beginning of a process in which his conscience summons him to his ownmost potentiality-for-Being-his-Self. One element of this summons of conscience is Hamlet's understanding of his need to act, even while possibly facing his own death. Such is the only way, he grasps, to counter the wickedness and to avenge the vile crimes committed in the royal court at Elsinore. He further recognizes that if he wishes to struggle so as to unconceal and bring into the open the truth about the evil people and evil doings that encompass him, he must stop procrastinating and play-acting. Heidegger's thinking suggests that, for Hamlet, such an understanding is the first step in answering the call of conscience and in responding to the summons to fulfill his ownmost potentiality-for-Being-his-Self.

The call of conscience is Dasein calling itself. Yet, Heidegger adds, the call is not something Dasein prepared or planned. It is often a call against Dasein's expectations and against its will; it comes from Dasein, and from beyond Dasein. Borrowing a term from the ontology of Gabriel Marcel, Heidegger's call of conscience should be termed a mystery. This call often emerges when Dasein finds itself in a unique state—when, in anxiety about its potentiality-for-Being, Dasein recognizes its basic homelessness in the world and faces the nothingness that may emerge in its relations with the world. In this state, Dasein rejects the "public conscience" which is the voice of the "They." Thus, personal conscience comes into being as the call of care of Dasein, when Dasein has decided to face its thrownness and is anxious about its potentiality-for-Being. Hamlet's cited soliloquy is such an unexpected call of conscience, in which he recognizes his basic homelessness in the world and decides courageously to face the nothingness that encompasses much of his Being-in-the-world. This unprepared call, this mystery, comes from Hamlet's Being-in-the-world and from beyond him.

Heidegger explains that the structure of Dasein's thrownness, and the nullity that is at the heart of thrownness, is the basis upon which the call of conscience summons Dasein to Being-guilty. This nullity includes the possibility of Dasein choosing freedom, which is the readiness to respond to an appeal. And the readiness to personally respond to an appeal divorces Dasein from the "They," while making possible its own Being-guilty. I will not elaborate on these ideas. I do wish to state, however, that Heidegger does not link Being-guilty to Being-with-Others. (Buber elaborates upon this point in his essay "What Is Man?" which is discussed in Chapter 11.) Heidegger discusses and describes Being-guilty as essentially a solitary relationship, a relation of Dasein to its own potentiality-for-Being-its-Self.

Once again, Hamlet's plight and decisions help to illuminate Heidegger's thinking. Faced with the terrible evil that he discovers at Elsinore, for three acts Hamlet procrastinates and playacts his own existence and anguish. He relentlessly plays with the loneliness of madness and with the madness that can accompany anguish and a deep loneliness. In the moment of revelation and conversion, expressed in the above citation, he suddenly considers himself guilty for not acting and becomes resolute.

There are other Shakespearean heroes, however, whose existence and choices constitute a questioning of Heidegger's thinking and statements. Consider, again, the existence and the choice of Juliet, who leaps into a deep innocent love for Romeo. Her trusting wonderful love of Romeo seems akin to what Plato called a sacred madness, which is a marvelous gift of the gods. Even if we accept Heidegger's locutions, still Juliet's deeds and decisions raise no few poignant questions.

Here are five such questions. Is it not true that Juliet, who hears the call of conscience to follow her love, firmly rejects the demands of the "They"? Does not Juliet know, to the depth of her Being, that she will be guilty if she does *not* follow her love? Consequently, is it not true that the existence, the thoughts, the freedom, and the choices of Juliet are, from the moment of her leap into her love for Romeo, linked to her Being-with-Romeo? Is not this Being-with-Romeo crucial for Juliet's attempts to fulfill her potentiality-for-Being-her-Self? Does not Juliet resolutely face her own death in order to be true to her love for Romeo? In support of these questions, especially concerning Juliet's facing her own death, I wish to remind the reader that Juliet says to Friar Lawrence, after her father decreed that she must marry Count Paris: "I long to die, if what thou speakest speak not of remedy" [act 4, scene 1].

It should be evident that the answer to all the questions that I posed in the above paragraph is yes. This answer indicates that, for Juliet, Being-with-Romeo is central to her existence and also an authentic response to her call of conscience. Furthermore, Juliet's love for Romeo is crucial to her rejecting the demands of the "They" and to her resolutely facing her own death. Thus, Juliet's love of Romeo, and her deeds and decisions that support this love, are problematic for the thinking of Heidegger. Specifically, the life of Shakespeare's Juliet suggests that Heidegger's emphasis on the solitude of Dasein in his discussions of Being-guilty and of the call of conscience—this emphasis on Dasein's solitude—is unjustified. It leads to a narrowing of the realm of human existence.

* * *

Heidegger next explains that, from an ontological perspective, the call of conscience and Dasein's Being-guilty, as he described these phenomena, underlie the everyday understanding of conscience. The anthropological, theological, and psychological presentations of conscience, he holds, are also founded on his descriptions of the call of conscience and of Being-guilty. The details of Heidegger's argument can be skipped, since they do not add to the theme of my inquiry. What is relevant is a major problem that emerges. In his quest to divorce the authentic call of conscience from the dictates of the "They," Heidegger pretty much ignores a person's social and political responsibilities and the links of these responsibilities to the call of conscience. Furthermore, he dismisses the problem of a good and an evil conscience as secondary, explaining that Good and Evil are founded upon his ontology of Dasein and upon the call of conscience that he described.

To clarify the validity of his approach, Heidegger would probably state that social and political responsibility are not primordial; they stem from the call of conscience to Dasein to realize its potentiality-for-Being-its-Self. But this response again shows that his ontology is primarily concerned with Dasein's relations to itself and to its own potentials. It should therefore not surprise us that Heidegger's presentation of everyday conscience sets aside, as ontologically irrelevant, both love and the good and the evil conscience. With this approach, you must also set aside the Good and the Evil that a person may do or may encounter in the world at large and in one's personal relations with Others with whom Dasein shares this world. Thus, in Heidegger's fundamental ontology, a person's interhuman, social, and political relations and responsibilities are much too often set aside. For Heidegger, these responsibilities seem to be mere offshoots of Dasein's potentiality-for-Being-its-Self.

Yet, Heidegger holds, the call of conscience can lead Dasein to an authentic potentiality for Being. Such seems to happen to Hamlet in the soliloquy presented earlier. The state of mind of anxiety accompanies the call. Dasein's discourse with the call of conscience, in which its Being-guilty is disclosed, is often a discourse in silence. For some persons there may be no alternative to silence, since words are frequently held captive by the so-called common sense, which is usually based upon the idle talk of the "They."

Heidegger calls the entire existential situation of responding to the call of conscience while facing one's own death resoluteness. Put differently, resoluteness is Dasein's readiness for anxiety while it silently projects itself upon its Being-guilty. Such resoluteness is the truth of Dasein; it frees Dasein from the dictates of the "They" and discloses, in bold relief, its own Being-in-the-world. Also, resoluteness may frequently encourage Dasein to be solicitous with other Daseins. Moreover, a resolute Dasein may attempt to encourage Others to become free and to fulfill their own potentiality-for-Being.

Dasein's resoluteness occurs at a particular time in a particular situation. In choosing to act resolutely, Dasein establishes a particular situation. This particular situation, in which Dasein discloses itself in resoluteness, differs from the general situation that the "They" knows, and in which Dasein frequently exists. General situations, dominated by the insidious dictates of the "They," rarely arouse anxiety. They have no direct link to Dasein's possible choice of resoluteness and to its existing authentically as care. When it is dominated by the "They," usually, every Dasein floats along quite placidly, tacitly accepting what the general situation discloses.

Once again, Hamlet's soliloquy exemplifies Heidegger's thinking. Probably many soldiers in Fortinbras's army vaguely recognize, as Hamlet puts it, that they may be going to their death for "a fantasy and trick of fame." Like the officer of their army who enlightens Hamlet on what is happening, it seems that Fortinbras's soldiers accept this general situation irresolutely; they float along with it. In contrast, Hamlet responds to these soldiers' placid acceptance of their sad plight, and to their general situation, with anxiety, authentically, and with a call of conscience which leads him to statements of resolution. In his soliloquy, Hamlet converts the general situation of Fortinbras's army into an anguished examination of his own life. He thus lucidly establishes his own particular situation; in response to this lucid seeing of his terrible situation, he determines to act resolutely.

However, this example again reveals Heidegger's emphasis on solitude and loneliness as necessary for choosing both resoluteness and one's particular situation. I skip showing again that such need not be the case. Suffice it to mention again that Shakespeare's Romeo and Juliet, whose loving relations I have discussed, and will often return to, share an anguished and wonderful particular situation in which care and resoluteness in facing one's own death prevail—together with a deep love of each other.

To comprehend the totality of Dasein, the links between its authentic anticipation of its own death and resoluteness, care, and its potentiality-for-Being-a-whole need to be clarified. Heidegger undertakes this task. He indicates that since Dasein's Being is conceived as care, his inquiry will help to clarify the phenomenon of care. Temporality will also be discussed, since it is experienced in a primordial way when Dasein authentically relates as a whole in anticipatory resoluteness. The fundamental structures of Dasein are temporal, hence understanding temporality casts much light on the Being of Dasein.

* * *

Heidegger's discussion of the phenomenon of Dasein's Being-guilty reveals a rather problematic approach. He holds that since there exists a call of conscience, guilt belongs to the Being of Dasein, and hence Dasein is essentially guilty. He emphasizes that he is describing Dasein's fundamental ontology, not its ethical or religious state. However, his description of Dasein accords very well with the Christian belief that, as a result of the fall of Adam, each and every human being is born guilty. Even without this similarity, Heidegger's description of Dasein's ontological state as essentially guilty is questionable. I find it especially questionable, since he provides no examples or descriptions that support his statement that guilt belongs to the Being of Dasein and that Dasein is essentially guilty. Nor does he provide any ontological grounds, beyond the existence of the call of conscience, for this sweeping ontological assertion.

The example of Hamlet shows that resoluteness—when it is defined as Dasein letting itself be called by conscience, which reveals its Being-guilty—is a significant possibility. At times, pursuing this possibility may lead to a better mode of existence. By letting himself be called by his conscience, Hamlet, at least, decides to stop procrastinating and quit playacting his own sad situation. The example also reveals that, as Heidegger suggests, Dasein can be transparent to its Being-guilty and can harbor in itself an authentic Being-toward-death, which is crucial for its choosing resoluteness. Yet I am not sure that even Hamlet's soliloquy, coupled with his subsequent deeds and statements, accord with the view that, for Dasein, Being-guilty is constant.

Counterexamples to Heidegger's statement that guilt belongs to the Being of Dasein are not difficult to find. The wonderful innocent love that engulfed Shakespeare's Romeo and Juliet could hardly come into being if Romeo and Juliet were essentially guilty. All worthy love, which as Plato repeatedly indicated leads to wisdom, will only come into being if the lovers are essentially innocent and whole. Additional examples of such an engulfing innocent love can be found in the novels of Tolstoy and Dostoyevsky, and in the poems of Edgar Allan Poe and Pablo Neruda. I discuss one such poem by Poe, "Annabel Lee," in Chapter 8. Elsewhere I have shown that Heidegger's later philosophy can help us learn from poetry how to relate wholly in love.[4]

From my experience, love such as is described by Neruda and Poe is not confined to literary works. Such love also may come into being in the life of a person who lives and acts wholly and who has the good fortune to meet a beloved to whom he or she can relate with one's entire Being. If the beloved also loves the lover, with his or her whole being, the peaks of love that poets describe can be attained—here and now. Thus, Heidegger's sweeping statement that Dasein is essentially guilty is, at best, very problematic. I would venture to argue that it is false.

Despite this problem, I agree with certain components of Heidegger's thinking on Dasein's facing its own death; these components are supported by the example of Hamlet. In brief, Dasein's resoluteness in facing its own death, coupled with its wanting-to-have-a-conscience, will often bring it to the resoluteness of taking action here and now. Heidegger adds that when it exists resolutely, Dasein will relate soberly to the difficult possibilities facing it. It is interesting that this sobriety is often accompanied by a joy in the existence of these possibilities. Living with resoluteness also frees Dasein from daily relating to the seducing curiosities of the world.

* * *

Heidegger notes that the care-structure is a condition for Dasein's Being-a-whole. Dasein's relation to Death, conscience, and guilt are all anchored in care. To illuminate care, he clarifies the existentiality of the Self, beginning from Dasein's saying "I" in its everyday understanding of itself.

In everyday discourse, the "I" is grasped as me and nothing else, as an absolute subject, as the same persisting something that is me. However, Heidegger believes, this ontical grasping of the "I" cannot be the basis of an ontological understanding. He adds that even Kant's description of the "I," or the "I think," as the basis of his transcendental subject of thoughts, does not bring the ontological foundation of the "I" to light. He rejects Kant's underlying view that the "I" is something present-at-hand. Kant's major problem was that he did not see the "I" as an "I-am-in-a-world"; he viewed the "I" ontically and did not comprehend that when Dasein says "I" it expresses itself as Being-in-the-world. The problem we face is that, like Kant, each Dasein usually views itself ontically and does not see itself as Being-in-the-world. Put differently, Dasein usually remains on the ontic level in which it flees from itself into the "They-self." As repeatedly stated, when such occurs, the "I" is dominated by the "They" and exists inauthentically.

Selfhood, Heidegger states, should not be presented as a subject or as a substance; it should be linked to Dasein's authentic potentiality-for-Being-one's-self. Dasein is ahead of itself in the world. Due to its being ahead of itself, it can authentically and resolutely face its own death and discover itself as care. Thus, the "I" is an entity for whom the issue of its own Being, now and in the future, is crucial. This ontological comprehending of the "I" is totally concealed when one views the "I" as a subject or a substance, in short, as something present-at-hand in universal time. These manners of comprehending the "I" are inauthentic. They prevail, however, because of the broad acceptance of the superficial manners of relating to beings, to Being, and to time, that are promoted by the "They."

Heidegger here presents the primordial link between Being and time, a link central to Dasein's existence and vital to his own thinking. When Dasein is resolute, it has "the unity of a future which makes present in the process of having been."[5] He calls this unity of Dasein's being in resoluteness: temporality. Once again Hamlet's state of existence and decisions, as expressed in the above soliloquy, fit Heidegger's description of the link between resoluteness and temporality. While deciding to struggle for honor and for justice in his present situation, Hamlet senses and expresses the need for unity in his future being; and by making that future present in his mind, he rejects the process by which he formerly did not undertake such a struggle.

The unity of Dasein's being helps to clarify the meaning of authentic care. Heidegger explains that authentic care is Dasein's attaining the unity of future, present, and past in resoluteness, a unity which he designated as temporality. He adds that when Dasein is resolute, it has brought itself back from falling into a mode of existence of ready-to-hand or present-at-hand beings, during which it accepts time that is governed by the dictates of the "They." With such a bringing itself back from falling, Dasein is there, authentically facing the future, present, and past with a clearer vision of the situation in which it finds itself and of its Being-in-the-world. This clear vision of its situation has been disclosed by Dasein's resoluteness and authenticity. Hamlet's soliloquy depicts his bringing of himself back from falling into procastrination and from living the ambiguity of playacting and idle talk into a much clearer vision of his difficult situation. The soliloquy also reveals his wish to live with authentic care through undertaking an authentic existence in time.

As against the accepted concept of time as a series of "nows," Heidegger views time as a unity of ecstases, that is, as a unity of instances of Dasein's going beyond itself. Dasein goes beyond itself in an ecstases either toward the future, or back to the past, or in encountering something in the present. In these ecstases, Dasein is outside itself, for itself. The ecstases directed toward future, present, and past are linked with each other and constitute temporality. Consequently, grasping time as a pure series of "nows" is inauthentic, it is a leveling down of the ecstases, and with it the Being of Dasein.

Primordial authentic temporality emerges in Dasein's relation to the future. Furthermore, through its relation to the future, Dasein determines whether its relations to the present and the past are authentic. Again, Heidegger does not give examples of his thoughts on ecstases and temporality. As already mentioned, enlightening examples can be found in great literature. Here is one such example.

In the chapter "Swann in Love" in *Remembrance of Things Past*, Marcel Proust shows in great detail how Swann's inauthentic manner of relating, both to his future with Odette and to his past love for her, infects his everyday existence.[6] Swann's ecstases toward an inauthentic future leads to his always grasping the present and his past inauthentically. This daily inauthenticity supports Swann's striving to believe in Odette's love, which, he knows, has vanished. This painful morass of inauthenticity is suddenly illuminated at a concert, when Swann suddenly hears the violin play a certain phrase from Vinteuil's sonata. Swann shudders, since he recognizes that it was precisely to this musical phrase that he and Odette would happily listen together when she still loved him.

But Swann soon brushes aside this stinging moment of lucidity, in which Odette's present indifference to him is harshly illuminated. He quickly abandons his agonizing memory, and with it the moment of revelation that stemmed from hearing the muscial phrase; he revives his inauthentic relation to the future. Swann's decisions accord with Heidegger's thinking. The key to an authentic existence, which Swann might have chosen but brushed aside, is not the authentic recognition of discrepancies between moments of the past and one's situation in the present. The key to an authentic existence is the specific ecstases toward the future that Dasein chooses.

Heidegger states categorically: "Care is Being-towards-death."[7] By this he means that authentic care emerges when Dasein exists finitely, when it faces its own death resolutely. This definition leads to the question of infinite time within which, supposedly, Dasein exists finitely.

How does infinite time arise? Heidegger suggests that it arises out of inauthentic temporality, which must be examined in Dasein's everyday existence. Put differently, if we wish to comprehend the source of so-called objective infinite time, the temporality of Dasein's inauthentic existence must be clarified. One aspect of this temporality is Dasein's reckoning with time, which is a result of Dasein relating to itself as using itself up in time. In this reckoning with time, Dasein frequently relates to itself as a ready-to-hand object, whose existence is governed by its being used in time. For instance, when institutions in society consider a person to be merely a human resource, existing solely for their use, as many large institutions do today, these institutions are relating to that person as a resource, or a ready-to-hand object. I return to this example in a later chapter.

The reckoning with time extends beyond Dasein's existence to those entities that are ready-to-hand and present-at-hand, endowing them also with an existence in time. Heidegger calls this endowed attribute of beings in the world within-time-ness. He holds within-time-ness to be the basis upon which the traditional concept of external time, which may be measured by clocks, arises. Our idea of infinite time is also supported by this reckoning. But here we see an interesting humanist approach emerging from Heidegger's discussion. The approach is expressed in his belief that the ontological source of Dasein's Being towers above what springs from it, including Dasein's reckoning with time. It also towers above all things that may arise from this reckoning, such as the idea of infinite time and utensils linked to time—say, atomic clocks.

* * *

Temporality, Heidegger holds, is central to the disclosedness of every aspect of Dasein's Being-in-the-world. Here I present only the direction of his thoughts, since they are quite marginal to the theme of my study. Central to the difference between authentic and inauthentic disclosedness, he suggests, is the distinction between anticipating the future and awaiting the future. Consider how this distinction relates to understanding. When Dasein anticipates the future, it is resolute, and this resolution leads it to understand what it encounters in relation to its potentiality-for-Being. Put succinctly, when Dasein is resolute and anticipates the future, while endeavoring to understand a situation, it brings forth its potentiality-for-Being. In contrast, when Dasein merely awaits the future, it is irresolute; it lets the terms of the "They" bring to itself an understanding of the situation in which it finds itself. Its understanding is inauthentic.

Consider, one final time in this chapter, the example of Hamlet. After meeting an officer in Fortinbras's army, Hamlet's understanding of his situation changed; he began to anticipate his future instead of merely awaiting the future. Hamlet's resoluteness and his anticipating of the future, while relating lucidly to his past and present, led to what Heidegger calls a "moment of vision." As in Hamlet's soliloquy, a "moment of vision" includes what Heidegger terms resolute rapture, which is an authentic understanding that cannot be clarified in terms of the "now." In contrast, inauthentic understanding of one's situation emerges when Dasein has forgotten itself in its thrown situation and irresolutely merely awaits the future.

In contrast to Hamlet, look again at the example of Proust's Swann, who chooses to be inauthentic. Swann's life is characterized by irresoluteness, especially in relation to his so-called love for Odette, who is indifferent to him. Forgetfulness of his thrown self, blended with merely awaiting the future and with an inauthentic understanding of his past and present, also characterizes Swann's life. Suddenly he hears again the phrase from Vinteuil's sonata—a phrase that he and Odette delighted in hearing together when she, supposedly, still loved him. This phrase leads to memories which reveal the banality, the self-deceit, and the daily misery of his current life, in which he merely awaits the future. Unfortunately, however, Swann emerges from his forgetting of the past and his inauthentic understanding for only a very short moment. He soon abandons the lucidity aroused by Vinteuil's sonata; Swann sinks back into irresolute existence and into his inauthentic understanding based on merely awaiting the future. These literary examples reveal that, as Heidegger indicated, merely awaiting the future is strongly linked to living

inauthentically, while anticipating the future can help a person live authentically.

In his discussion of the temporality of Dasein's moods or states of
mind, Heidegger returns to the distinction between fear and anxiety.
Fear is based on forgetfulness of one's being thrown and on awaiting
something threatening. In contrast, anxiety brings one face to face with
one's being thrown and thus opens Dasein to the possibility of resolution
and of courageous anticipation. Other moods, such as indifference, can
also be characterized in terms of ecstases; indifference, for instance, is an
abandoning of oneself to one's thrownness in time.

I skip Heidegger's presentation of the temporality of curiosity, as an
example of the temporality of Dasein's falling. He concludes his discussion of the temporality of Dasein's disclosedness with the observation
that discourse articulates Dasein's understanding, states of mind, and
falling. Hence, discourse makes present the temporality of Dasein's disclosedness. In addition, discourse itself is temporal, since all conversation
between Daseins is grounded on the ecstatical unity of Dasein's temporality.

It is sad to discover that in his discussion of temporality in the disclosedness of Dasein, Heidegger never mentions other Daseins. In this
section, Being-with seems to have vanished from Dasein's Being-in-the-
world. Why? I do not know.

Heidegger's ignoring of Dasein's Being-with continues when he turns
to discussing the temporality of Dasein's circumspective concern and its
unique ability to develop a theoretical attitude on the basis of this concern. These thoughts are hardly significant for the theme of my study,
and hence I do not present them. I do wish to point out, however, that
central to Heidegger's detailed discussion of the temporality of circumspective concern, and of the role of temporality in the development of
the theoretical attitude, is Dasein's temporal and manipulating relation
to equipment, to those things that are ready-to-hand. I wish once more
to emphasize that, in this discussion, there is no reference to Dasein's
relations with other Daseins. In the context of his discussions on theory,
Heidegger's ignoring of Dasein as Being-with is, again, quite surprising.
Heidegger knew very well that the development and spreading of a theoretical attitude requires that Dasein share its observations with other
Daseins. In short, any theory is established on the basis of Dasein's
Being-with and his sharing of his thoughts with other Daseins.

Someone may ask, Why are you surprised at Heidegger's not discussing Being-with? You explained that his fundamental ontology is based
on the ecstases of temporality, which are a manner of being of each
Dasein. From your explanation it is evident that in these ecstases Dasein
is alone in its relation to its future, its past, and its present, to equipment

and to the world. What justifies your saying that Heidegger surprises you?

These questions lead to the problem at the core this book: the status of the I–Thou. But since Heidegger's thinking during the period that he criticized the I–Thou has not yet been presented fully, I can only partially suggest the linkage between my surprise and the temporality presented in *Being and Time*.

For Heidegger, it should have been clear that in all stages of his presenting a fundamental ontology, he must be able to account for the fullness of human existence; this fullness includes, as he stated, existing with other Daseins. Thus, it *is* surprising that Heidegger's account of temporality and ecstases does not relate to this fullness, nor to the many diverse manners in which Dasein exists in time with other Daseins. Thus, it repeatedly surprises me that, in his account of temporality, Heidegger seems unable to relate to those enhancing and often euphoric moments of Being-with another Dasein, which many persons have testified as being of great worth in their life. I have repeatedly mentioned those marvelous moments of love, or friendship, in which time seemed to stop. I can only conclude that temporality and the ecstases as described by Heidegger, provide only a partial basis for Dasein's Being-in-the-world.

* * *

In the closing chapters of *Being and Time*, Heidegger emphasizes that through temporalizing itself, Dasein sets the horizons of the world and is essentially in a world. He adds that the world is neither ready-to-hand nor present-at-hand; it is neither a series of pieces of equipment nor a random collection of entities, be they quarks, genomes, particles of cosmic dust, or cabbages and kings. Since temporality is essential for the establishment of a world, without Dasein existing there is no world. Thus, what Heidegger calls "the ecstatico-horizontal unity of temporality"[8] is the basis of comprehending and understanding Dasein as Being-in-the-world.

The question arises, if Dasein's temporality is essential for the establishment of a world, what is its relation to space? I have already pointed out that, for Heidegger, Dasein is not primarily an object in space, something present-at-hand. The possibility of viewing Dasein as an object in space emerges after Dasein has established its relation to space. Dasein establishes its relation to space through its establishing a world and making room for itself in space by its directionality and by its de-severence of entities. Almost always, such a making room for itself in space needs equipment. The atronomer studying a star in Orion directs the telescope to the star and de-severs it. By these acts the astronomer makes room for his or her self in cosmic space. The astronomer also takes this space in, into his or her being, and can then convey his or her findings to others. But this making room for space is based on temporality, on the ecstases of Dasein, by which it establishes a future, a past, and a present. Indeed, the astronomer's vocation exemplifies this making room for space on the basis of temporality. When he or she remarks, say, that a star in Orion is two hundred light-years away, the space established is founded upon Dasein's temporality.

I must add, however, that the space that Heidegger describes has little to do with the space that may arise between persons. For such a space to arise, a space which Buber calls "the between," a relationship of mutuality and genuine sharing between two persons must come into being. Put succinctly, the space of "the between," which Heidegger quite blatantly ignores, may be established by two persons who wish to share their being with each other.

The last two chapters of *Being and Time* deal with topics that have little relevance for the question concerning the status of the I–Thou. Hence, I shall only mention the topics discussed. In these chapters, Heidegger shows how his fundamental ontology can help to clarify Dasein as a historical being, and how his thinking on Dasein's temporality serves as a source for the ordinary everyday conception of time. No mention is made in these chapters of the possibility of a different manner of living time, or of temporalizing that can emerge in worthy relations between Dasein and Dasein. In the final chapter of *Being and Time*, being with Others is described as Dasein maintaining itself in a public and average intelligibility.[9]

I can categorically conclude that time, as it is lived by many persons who establish genuine dialogue and profound worthy human relations with Others, is not discussed in *Being and Time*. Nor is the possibility of what Buber calls speaking the primary word *Thou*, in which time stands still, included in Heidegger's presentation and discussion of time.

NOTES

1. Martin Heidegger, *Being and Time*, trans. John Macquarrie and Edward Robinson (Oxford, Eng.: Basil Blackwell, 1962), p. 294.

2. Ibid., p. 306.

3. Ibid., p. 312.

4. Haim Gordon, *Dwelling Poetically: Educational Challenges in Heidegger's Writings on Poetry* (Amsterdam: Rodopi, 2000).

5. Heidegger, *Being and Time*, p. 374.

6. Marcel Proust, *Remembrance of Things Past*, trans. C. K. Scott Moncrieff (New York: Random House, 1934), pp. 144–292.

7. Heidegger, *Being and Time*, p. 378.

8. Ibid., p. 418.

9. Ibid., p. 463.

Section B: Heidegger's Rejection of the I–Thou

Chapter 4

Phenomenology and Dasein

Heidegger's book *The Basic Problems of Phenomenology* is the text of a lecture course that he taught at the University of Marburg in the summer semester of 1927.[1] More than four and a half decades passed before a book was published on the basis of these lectures. In composing the book, Heidegger's typewritten text of the lectures, which included his insertions and marginalia, was supplemented by a transcription of the lectures written in 1927 by a student in the course, Simon Moser. The book came out in Germany in 1975, the year Heidegger died. As I have indicated in the Introduction, in this book Heidegger briefly criticizes the I–Thou. I am not very happy with the English translation; hence, in what follows, I will, at times, cite the original German and provide my translation.

The question raised at the beginning of the book is, What is the appropriate topic of philosophy? After rejecting a few topics and approaches which are commonly associated with philosophy, Heidegger writes: *"Das Sein ist das echte und einzige Thema der Philosophie,"* which I translate: Being is the genuine and sole theme of philosophy.[2] This statement accords, of course, with the opening remarks of *Being and Time*. He concludes that philosophy is the science of Being. His book may be considered to be an introduction to this science, both a historical and a phenomenological introduction.

Yet the novelty of Heidegger's approach is what he calls his phenomenological way of dealing with the topics of this science. As in *Being and Time*, he states that the way that leads to the science of Being must be linked to a fundamental ontology of Dasein. It is evident that Dasein's understanding of Being—albeit a vague and stuttering understanding—makes possible its comportment toward beings. For instance, without some understanding of Being, Heidegger holds, Dasein could not use the copula "is" in everyday discourse. Consequently, the science of Being presupposes an analytic of Dasein which will disclose its fundamental ontology. Before turning to the science of Being, Heidegger very briefly reiterates his finding that was spelled out in *Being and Time*: Dasein's Being is temporality, and therefore time is the horizon from which Being may become intelligible. He discusses Dasein's relation to time in part 2 of *The Basic Problems of Phenomenology*.

Much of the book deals with Heidegger's attempt to illuminate Being by examining certain instances in the history of human thinking on Being. For all that, the book is no mere historical survey. At times, Heidegger adds valuable insights to his historical presentation by providing a phenomenological perspective on and analysis of certain historical approaches to thinking on Being. Discussing all these valuable insights, however, would lead us astray from the theme of my study. Hence, I will concentrate briefly on those sections in which, I believe, Heidegger adds depth to his fundamental ontology of Dasein, as presented in my discussion of *Being and Time*. Moreover, my discussion will focus primarily on Heidegger's thoughts and insights which have some relevance for understanding his conclusions concerning the status of the I–Thou.

* * *

Part 1 of *The Basic Problems of Phenomenology* is "Critical Phenomenological Discussion of Some Traditional Theses about Being." Chapter 1 is "Kant's Thesis: Being Is Not a Real Predicate." The chapter deals primarily with Kant's thinking on Being, which is very much based on the primacy of perception in Dasein's relating to reality. The chapter also includes a discussion on intentionality, which adds breadth and depth to Heidegger's presentation of Dasein in *Being and Time*.

Heidegger introduces the concept of intentionality as central to Dasein's comporting itself toward beings; he defines intentionality as a directing toward. Dasein's being directs itself toward beings, especially in the case of perception. Yet Heidegger wants to discover and to present the structure of intentionality and how it is grounded in Dasein's constitution. He begins by rejecting the naïvely accepted position that intentionality is an extant, or external, relation between two extant beings. Put otherwise, he rejects the notion that it is a relation between a psychical subject that relates intentionally to a physical object. According to the naïve position, the physical object is the reason that the psychical subject comports itself intentionally.

Heidegger holds that this naïve position misses both the nature and the mode of being of intentionality. It is mistaken because the external physical object is ontologically secondary to the structure of intentionality, which is essential to the Being of Dasein. Put differently, intentionality does not occur because a subject encounters an object. There is not a subject or an ego which in certain instances relates intentionally. Rather, Dasein's Being is intentional. Heidegger states clearly: "the subject is structured intentionally within itself. As subject it is directed toward."[3]

He supports this statement by considering hallucinations; for instance, when someone sees elephants walking around in this room even though no such elephants are present. These hallucinations are instances of intentionality without a physical object being present and extant—there definitely are no elephants in this room. Heidegger concludes that perceiving, as such, is intentional, whether Dasein perceives existing or imaginary objects. Hence, intentionality, as central to perceiving, is intrinsic to Dasein as a self-comporting subject. Intentionality belongs to Dasein's existence; it constitutes Dasein's different modes of existence.

Heidegger adds that a correct understanding of intentionality also helps elucidate Dasein's relationship to transcendence. Since Dasein is structured intentionally, it is oriented toward the extant, toward the physical object as a whole. Consequently, by relating intentionally Dasein relates toward objects transcendentally, that is, it relates to the whole object which is always beyond its specific perceptions. Heidegger states, "it is precisely intentionality and nothing else in which *transcendence* exists."[4] Here is an important point for Heidegger's fundamental ontology: through Dasein's being structured intentionally, transcendence comes into being for Dasein.

The linkage between intentionality and transcendence is not difficult to discern. Heidegger points out that when I perceive something I do not direct myself toward sensations, but rather toward objects which transcend my immediate experience. As already explained in previous chapters, I do not see colors and forms, but this red cup or that green sheet of paper. I do not hear mere sounds. Rather, I listen to the patter of rain on the windowpane or to the loud horn of the truck driving up the street. I do not perceive mere odors; rather, I smell the pungency of onions frying on the stove or the sweetness of the desert air after a first rain. Since I always perceive objects, my perceptions are always intertwined with intentionality. Thus, while perceiving the objects that I intend, their transcendence becomes evident.

As Heidegger states, this brief description of intentionality undermines many philosophical and psychological positions. Consider the two major points that he makes, that intentionality is not an external relation between a psychical subject and a physical object, and that the intentional constitution of Dasein conditions transcendence. These findings throw doubt on the traditional understanding of the psychical subject as an isolated entity which establishes relations with the world. This traditional understanding of the psychical subject, which in modern philosophy has roots in assumptions and assertions formulated by Descartes, is still accepted by many psychologists, such as Sigmund Freud, Carl Jung, and their followers. It is also accepted by no few thinkers, for instance, those philosophers who espouse pragmatism or analytic philosophy. A more direct result of Heidegger's discussion is that psychology, as a positive science, which assumes an independent subject, has been shown to have been unaware of the ontology of the subject that it assumes. Therefore, many of the findings and conclusions of positive psychology are frequently problematical, and, at times, false.

It is quite surprising to find that Heidegger does not discuss intentionality in relation to other people. What happens when I direct myself intentionally toward, say, my daughter, who may decide to direct herself toward me? Is there an interaction of intentionalities?

These and other questions concerning intentionality and human relations do not arise in this chapter, which is dedicated to Kant's thinking on Being. In this chapter, it seems that Heidegger's main concern is to show that intentionality is central to Dasein's being and to emphasize the mistake of confining intentionality within the limits of the subject–object model. His arguments also strive to erode the validity of the subject–object model. He does not attempt to elucidate intentionality, or to think about it, say, in the context of noninstrumental relationships between persons. Nor does a fundamental discussion of intentionality, which includes Being-with other persons, emerge later in the book.

Someone may suggest that the reason that, in chapter 1, Heidegger describes intentionality only in relation to instrumentality and thingness is that his thinking is directed toward elucidating the question of Being. This suggestion is supported by the fact that in the final pages of the chapter he attempts to clarify the link between intentionality and Kant's presentation of perception, on one hand, and beings that are extant or ready-to-hand, on the other. Such a clarification, he believes, brings us closer to comprehending and formulating possible responses to the question of Being. My inquiry concerning the status of the I–Thou does not require that we follow Heidegger's thinking in this direction.

However, despite the enlightening findings of Heidegger in his thinking about intentionality and transcendence, there is no assurance that by overlooking the interhuman aspects of perception and of intentionality a thinker can better respond to the question of Being. Might not the opposite be the case? Couldn't someone argue that, to come closer to comprehending Being, we should carefully clarify and elucidate the ontology of the interhuman aspects of Dasein's intentionality? In my careful readings of his texts, I never found that Heidegger considered such questions.

* * *

Part 1, chapter 2 of *The Basic Problems of Phenomenology* is "The Thesis of Medieval Ontology Derived from Aristotle: To the Constitution of the Being of a Being There Belong Essence and Existence." The representatives of medieval thinking on Being that are discussed by Heidegger are Thomas Aquinas, Duns Scotus, and Francisco Suarez. He briefly presents their thoughts on the relation between essence and existence in beings. What is significant for the theme of my study is his phenomenological clarification of their writings on Being. Heidegger suggests that in order to throw light on the concepts "essence" and "existence," as understood by these medieval thinkers, he needs to show that these concepts are derived from what he calls the *"productive comportment of Dasein."*[5]

For a moment, let us look at Heidegger's suggestion in an oversimplified manner. Kant, true to the philosophical tradition since Descartes, developed his thinking in relation to beings and Being on the basis of Dasein as perceiving. In contrast, the medieval thinkers, true to the Aristotelian tradition which then prevailed, developed their thinking in relation to beings and Being based on Dasein as producing. This manner of looking is oversimplified because, as the above-mentioned medieval thinkers knew very well, in Dasein's existence perception and producing very often blend. Here, however, Heidegger is primarily showing a difference in emphasis between the two approaches to thinking about beings and Being.

In the final pages of the chapter, Heidegger brings up a problem linked to the distinction between essence and existence and crucial to the fundamental ontology of Dasein. The essence of a being is its whatness, which is distinguished from its existence. Thus, the essence of a thing is supposed to answer the question, What is this specific thing? Usually we can find the answer to this question for the many entities that we encounter in the world by relying on common sense, or on scientific research, literature, and discourse. We may also find answers to such a question in works of art and in daily discussions with others. From common sense, we know what a table is, even if there is not a table in this room. We can describe the whatness of centaurs even if they do not exist and never have existed. Yet, Heidegger points out, there is a unique problem when we attempt to relate to the essence of Dasein. As a being among other beings, Dasein cannot be interrogated by the question, What is this? Heidegger explains: "The Dasein is not constituted by whatness but—if we may coin the expression—by *whoness*. The answer does not give a thing but an I, you, we."[6]

Hence the relationship of essence and existence, and its link to what-ness, becomes problematic, since it does not hold when we discuss persons, when we discuss you and me. The stating of this problem has brought forth some clarifying philosophical responses. Jean-Paul Sartre, for instance, responded to this problem by stating his well-known explanation:

there is at least one being whose existence comes before its essence, a being which exists before it can be defined by any conception of it. That being is man or, as Heidegger has it, the human reality.[7]

In this citation, Sartre's conclusion pretty much accords with Heidegger's thinking. Sartre explains that we learn *who* a person is through that person's daily decisions and actions, in short, through a person's way of living his or her freedom.

After posing the problem in chapter 2, Heidegger does not proceed as rapidly as Sartre. He makes no attempt to broadly address or to unravel the implications arising from Dasein being constituted by "whoness." For instance, he does not ponder the different relationships that can come into existence between two or more Daseins and how certain and specific relationships may affect the "whoness" of each Dasein. Heidegger does state categorically that when relating to beings, in addition to essence and existence, we must acknowledge that there also exists the "whoness" of Dasein. He adds that Dasein's "whoness," with all its implications and manifestations, was quite ignored by medieval philosophers and later also by Descartes and by the thinkers in the Cartesian tradition. He does not pursue the implications of this finding, as I say, probably because the topic that mainly concerned Heidegger was the phenomenological inquiry of Being.

* * *

Part 1, chapter 3 of *The Basic Problems of Phenomenology* is "The Thesis of Modern Ontology: The Basic Ways of Being Are the Being of Nature (Res Extensa) and the Being of Mind (Res Cogitans)." While turning to modern ontology, Heidegger again reiterates a point central to his thinking: any ontological inquiry concerning Being must relate to and assess the being of Dasein. This point probably was one reason that led to his choosing to begin the chapter with a discussion of the thinking of Kant, whose reflections upon the ego and orientation toward the subject are representative of modern ontology. Another reason may have been his decision to challenge the tenets of some of the neo-Kantians, whose thinking was prominent in Germany in that period.

Heidegger hurries to point out that in all modern philosophy, including in Kant's writings, there is a problem—modern philosophy's orientation toward the subject has little to do with the fundamental ontology of Dasein. The presentation of Kant's three perspectives of the conception of the ego help Heidegger to clarify this ontological lack in modern philosophy.

Heidegger presents these three perspectives of Kant's conception of the ego separately. The first perspective is that of the transcending personality, the ego who thinks, perceives, judges, loves, hates, strives, and relates in many other ways. In these manners of relating to the world, even though a person may be fully involved in, say, thinking or hating, the I is always present. Thus, the ego is a subject endowed with self-consciousness, while acting in the world. Put differently, in addition to our assigning predicates—such as loving, thinking, or hating—to the ego, the ego differs from other beings to which we assign predicates in being conscious of doing what the predicates determine. When I love Rivca, or when Matilde Urrutia thinks about the poetry of Pablo Neruda, or when Eduardo hates Henry Kissinger and his evil deeds, I know that I am loving, Matilde knows that she is thinking, and Eduardo knows that he is hating. The ego knows itself as the ground of loving, thinking, hating and of all its other compartments. The ego is the unity and the ground of these different manifestations.

Look closely, however, at this ego that is a unity and the ground of manifestations. In daily existence, we do not encounter an ego, but only manifestations, such as Haim loving Rivca, or Matilde thinking about Neruda's poetry, or Eduardo hating Henry Kissinger. The concept of the person, or of the ego, is a synthesis of the I that accompanies these manifestations. Through the unity of its self-consciousness, the ego transcends the daily manifestations attributed to it. Heidegger formulates the ontological result, using Kantian terms: "Das Ich als ursprüngliche synthesische Einheit der Apperzeption ist die ontologische Grundbedingung für alles Sein."[8] I translate this sentence thus: The ego, as the original synthetic unity of apperception, is the ontological fundamental condition for all Being.

Note that Heidegger's statement asserts clearly that Kant's ideas on the transcendental ego are not mere epistemology as the Neo-Kantian, and later, the philosophical analysis schools of thought suggested. Instead, Heidegger's interpretation, which seems well supported, indicates that Kant's presentation of the ego, as the fundamental condition for all Being, is very similar to the description of Dasein in *Being and Time*. In a word, Kant also describes the ontology of the ego.

As indicated, the transcendental personality is but one perspective of Kant's conception of personality. Kant's second perspective is that of personality as a psychological object, which can be studied by the inner sense. This perspective of the ego provides a foundation for many areas of scientific psychology and of philosophy. The psychological research and the theories proposed by Freud, Jung, and Alfred Adler are examples of studying personality as an empirical psychological object. These founders of contemporary psychology studied the ego as an empirical object on the basis of inner apprehension of its feelings, its links to its developing body, its thinking, its initiatives, its responses, and, in general, its manners of relating to other egos in the world. In addition, Jean-Paul Sartre and Maurice Merleau-Ponty, to give just two examples, published philosophical studies of personality, which were based on their studying personality by the inner sense.

According to Heidegger, Kant's third perspective of personality is that of the moral person, who is a responsible and accountable being. Being responsible requires a peculiar kind of self-consciousness, established on the basis of a moral feeling. Kant holds this moral feeling to be respect for the law, and also a person's respect for oneself as respecting the law. The law that a person should morally respect is the categorical imperative. (I assume Kant's formulation of this imperative to be well known.) You respect the categorical imperative, Kant holds, by acting daily in accordance with its guidance and its demands. On the basis of the moral personality, which is unique to humans, Kant reaches an ontological conclusion concerning humanity: each person is an end in itself, never a means. Even for God, a person is not a means, but an end. Hence, as one of Kant's formulations of the categorical imperative states, each person should grasp himself or herself as an end and relate to every other person as an end in a kingdom of ends.

For Heidegger, however, this ontological conclusion does not suffice; it says too little about the Being of the person to whom we should relate as an end. Heidegger states categorically: In the Cartesian tradition, in Kant's thinking, and in the thinking of the philosophers who followed him, the question of the Being of Dasein was not raised. Hence, any discussion of these thinkers contributes little to Heidegger's attempts to present a fundamental ontology. To show the direction for pursuing such a fundamental ontology, Heidegger once again discusses intentionality. He concludes that what thinkers since Descartes did not discuss, and what they probably did not see, is that "Intentionality belongs to the existence of the Dasein."[9]

Thus, Dasein always exists as a being that relates intentionally to other beings; furthermore, by relating intentionally, Dasein partially unveils these beings as beings. As noted, this relating intentionally constitutes the world with all its beings. Because I relate intentionally, a series of musical tones which I hear is not grasped as a mere series of harmonical sounds but is unveiled as one of the beautiful melodies in Mozart's Thirty-ninth Symphony. Because I relate intentionally, I do not see an elongated small narrow black form upon a large square brown background, but rather, I immediately perceive and unveil my black pen, sitting there on my brown wooden desk.

Heidegger now adds that the self is disclosed in intentional relations and accompanies all intentionality. "The self is there for the Dasein itself without reflection and without inner perception, *before* all reflection."[10] Reflection may help me to apprehend my self, but that self is already disclosed in the intentional relation that is prior to reflection. Hence, a person is what he or she pursues, struggles for, cares for, attempts to accomplish. A person discovers its self, its "I" in these and many other intentional decisions and activities. Each Dasein will understand itself by starting from its cares, struggles, pursuits, and daily acts and activities.

However, the above statement can mislead. Because Heidegger's mention of Dasein's pursuits and of cares has little to do with interhuman relations. Nor do these pursuits and cares have anything to do with the pursuit of justice. He views Dasein primarily as being a user of equipment, and its intentionality is, therefore, primarily directed toward the use of equipment. Hence his conclusion: "the Dasein finds itself primarily in things."[11]

Thus, Heidegger holds that each Dasein's self is reflected to that Dasein from the things with which it is concerned in everyday life, the things that it daily encounters. He adds that fully explaining this statement is beyond his present task, and hence his explanation will be partial and limited. As in *Being and Time*, he commences by showing that Dasein's ontological constitution is Being-in-the-world. By Being-in-the-world, each Dasein establishes an equipmental contexture in which it exists. The shoemaker's equipmental contexture—which includes awl, leather, hammer, nails, thread—is very different from the equipmental contexture of the airline pilot, and both of these differ from the equipmental contexture of the professor of chemistry or of the homeless beggar. Each particular Dasein, as Being-in-the-world, encounters itself and finds itself primarily in the things that are linked together in its own equipmental contexture.

* * *

In a striking insight, which appears before he summarizes chapter 3, Heidegger shows that even the poet's Being-in-the-world accords with his phenomenological approach. The poet uses words to unconceal beings and to disclose aspects of human existence; this engagement reveals to each poet, together with the beings that his poetry brings forth from concealment, his or her own self. Furthermore, often the dedicated reader of poetry may learn from the unconcealing of beings that emerges in the verses of poetry certain important truths about his or her own self. As an example, Heidegger cites a rather long section from Rainer Maria Rilke's poetic novel *The Notebooks of Malte Laurids Brigge*.[12]

In the cited section, the poet, Malte, encounters a last standing wall that was once part of an apartment house. The house is slowly being demolished. In this encounter, the daily, banal, and at times bizarre life of the people who inhabited the house before its destruction springs out to meet Malte. This life of the inhabitants of the house springs out from the broken plumbing, from the discolored paint, from the peeling wall-paper, from the traces of stains. The example indicates, Heidegger holds, that through his sensitivity to the equipmental contexture of other Das-eins as Beings-in-the-world, the poet shows us how the world and Being-in-the-world "leap toward us from the things."[13]

In this context, I wish to repeat a point already mentioned. From Hei-degger's statements, and from his presentation of a phenomenological fundamental ontology, we learn that Dasein finds itself in things, and how this finding of itself occurs. In Heidegger's presentation, however, there is no mention of the possibility of Dasein finding itself through profound relations and worthy intercourse with other persons. In Hei-degger's phenomenological fundamental ontology, other persons seem to exist on the far horizon of Dasein's Being-in-the-world. Hence, Hei-degger's writings suggest, other pesons hardly participate in Dasein's finding of itself.

Heidegger's choice of the citation from *The Notebooks of Malte Laurids Brigge* supports the barren aspects of the ontology of human existence and of interhuman relations that he presented. In this novel, which is a poignant description of what has been recorded in Malte's poetic and fantasy-oriented notebooks, you will seek in vain genuine relations of sharing between persons. Nowhere in the two-hundred-odd pages of this poetic novel does Rilke describe generous, or dialogical, or loving human relations. Indeed, given the wasteland of interhuman relations depicted in the novel, it is not surprising that Malte finds and unconceals truths about his self primarily in the things that he encounters. Malte's sad encounter with the last standing wall of a demolished house that Hei-degger cites is a mere example of the widespread social desolation de-scribed in the novel. It also testifies to the profound interhuman alienation of Malte, and of his sad aloneness—which the novel repeat-edly portrays.

Now we can ask, Is it not possible that Heidegger's choice of a literary example reveals problems inherent to the fundamental ontology that he presented? Is it not telling, that in order to reveal how Dasein finds itself primarily in things, Heidegger did not choose, say, a blues singer finding himself in his guitar and in the songs that he sings, or a painter finding herself in her brushes, canvas, easel, and paintings? Is it not telling that to show how Dasein finds itself in things, Heidegger chose an example of an alienated, sad, unfulfilled poet, Malte, finding himself in a last standing wall of a demolished apartment house?

Despite my criticism of this example, and despite the limitations that this example reveals about Heidegger's fundamental ontology, I should repeat a fact that has already been mentioned: I have found Heidegger's writings, especially his later writings, to be very enlightening in suggesting how to teach great poetry. Among the examples of great poetry that I would choose to teach and share with students, in accordance with Heidegger's insights, are poems that describe and reveal the beauty and the spirituality of interhuman relations. I have briefly presented and discussed Heidegger's worthy insights on this theme in a recent book.[14]

* * *

Part 1, chapter 4 of *The Basic Problems of Phenomenology* is "The Thesis of Logic: Every Being, Regardless of Its Particular Way of Being, Can Be Addressed and Talked About by Means of the 'Is.' The Being of the Copula." In a lengthy opening section of this chapter, which I skip, Heidegger very briefly presents the various ways major thinkers in the history of Western philosophy understood the copula, the "is," and its relation to beings and Being. He concentrates on the thinking of Aristotle, Thomas Hobbes, John Stewart Mill, and Hermann Lotze. On the basis of his historical survey, Heidegger concludes that a much more radical inquiry is needed: Any search for understanding the copula and its relation to beings and to Being should be linked to the phenomenological problem of assertion.

An assertion, Heidegger explains, is a manner by which Dasein communicates to other Daseins a determination about something that is displayed. An example can be the assertion "This window is dirty." In this assertion the specific window to which I am pointing, a window that is displayed and can be comprehended by some of my fellow Daseins, is determined to be unclean, say, covered with soot. Heidegger defines assertion as "communicatively determinant exhibition."[15] Intimated in this definition is the insight that in order for an assertion to determine and to exhibit something, Dasein must have unveiled, or uncovered, or unconcealed a being and communicated its finding to other Daseins. Consequently, an assertion discloses that a specific being, say, the dirt on the window, has been unveiled, or brought forth to our attention. Here, as in *Being and Time*, Heidegger goes beyond the belief that an assertion is true if it accords with facts. No, an assertion is true if it determines and exhibits a being that has been unconcealed or unveiled. As already pointed out, the Greek term for unconcealedness, *aletheia*, describes Heidegger's understanding of truth.

Heidegger's thoughts here add depth to our understanding of the role of language and of communication; they also partially illuminate Dasein's role in relation to beings and Being. *Being and Time* pointed out that when Dasein is under the sway of the "They," its Being is inauthentic and irresolute. For instance, language and communication are dominated by the "They" and hence characterized by idle talk, curiosity, and ambiguity. Now we comprehend better why these are distorted, and at times, destructive modes of communication. They are distorted because they are not concerned with disclosing or unveiling important truths about beings that have been brought forth from concealment. Instead, idle talk, curiosity, and ambiguity are manners by which Dasein plays games with itself and with other Daseins, by repeating and promoting superficial pronouncements. Unfortunately, these superficial pronouncements will often satisfy many a person's curiosity or craving for novelty; hence, they are frequently accepted by all and sundry. Often these superficial pronouncements are buttressed by insignificant truths and by half-truths.

From Heidegger's discussion of the copula, we can learn that worthy communication is firmly linked to truth, to Dasein's intentional unveiling of beings, to its intentional bringing forth of beings from concealment. Language, in which the copula has a crucial role, is therefore central to Dasein's unveiling of beings; it is crucial for Dasein's Being-in-the-world because it is necessary for the pursuit of truth. But, as mentioned, for truth to be accepted it must be shared. Dasein must be able to communicate the truth that it has unveiled to other Daseins. It must be able to show other Daseins the Being or beings that it has brought forth from concealment by its manner of Being-in-the-world. It is evident that language is crucial for communication of truth, for sharing the unveiling of beings with other Daseins. Thus, language is necessary for the unveiling of beings. Language is also necessary to help Dasein share with fellow Daseins its act of unveiling, what emerges in this unveiling, and its care for the Being of the beings that it has unveiled.

Looking back, we can consider what has happened in this final chapter of part 1 of Heidegger's book. Through his somewhat detailed and abstruse discussion of the role of the copula, and of its link to Being, Heidegger has shown a most important feature of the fundamental ontology of Dasein. This fundamental ontology includes the intentional unveiling of beings and the discovery and communication of truth. He also has shown that the existence of truth is linked to the Being of Dasein. So that there should be no mistake, Heidegger states clearly: without Dasein, truth could not come into being. In a few well-argued paragraphs, which I will not present, Heidegger convincingly counters all possible attacks that such views are mere subjectivist ramblings.

Heidegger concludes chapter 4, and part 1 of his book, with the observation that his phenomenological investigations have disclosed the complexities that can emerge when we attempt to raise the question of Being. He holds that part 1, at least partially, has made the question of Being a bit more accessible to us. I fully agree; Heidegger's thoughts are indeed enlightening. He also believes that he has presented, quite clearly, a few aspects of his fundamental ontological interpretation of Dasein. I again agree, and I again hold that these aspects are indeed enlightening, since they reveal important truths about the Being of Dasein.

In order to comprehend and learn from this interpretation of Dasein, so as to better investigate the question of Being, Heidegger turns to part 2 of his lecture course. However, there is a problem—he never completed part 2. In the sole chapter of part 2 which he presented in his lecture course, Heidegger turns to a discussion of Dasein's relation to time and temporality. In that discussion, his first critique of the I–Thou is presented.

NOTES

1. Martin Heidegger, *The Basic Problems of Phenomenology*, trans. Albert Hofstadter (Bloomington: Indiana University Press, 1982).

2. Martin Heidegger, *Die Grundprobleme der Phänomenologie* (Frankfurt am Main: Vittorio Klostermann, 1975), p. 15. Italics in original text.

3. Heidegger, *Basic Problems*, p. 60.

4. Ibid., p. 63.

5. Ibid., p. 105.

6. Ibid., p. 120.

7. Jean-Paul Sartre, *Existentialism and Humanism*, trans. Philip Mairet (London: Methuen, 1948), p. 28.

8. Heidegger, *Grundprobleme*, p. 181.

9. Heidegger, *Basic Problems*, p. 157.

10. Ibid., p. 159.

11. Ibid.

12. Rainer Maria Rilke, *The Notebooks of Malte Laurids Brigge*, trans. Stephen Mitchell (New York: Vintage Books, 1985), pp. 45–48.

13. Heidegger, *Basic Problems*, p. 173.

14. Haim Gordon, *Dwelling Poetically: Educational Challenges in Heidegger's Thinking on Poetry* (Amsterdam: Rodopi, 2000).

15. Heidegger, *Basic Problems*, p. 120.

Chapter 5

Heidegger's First Critique of the I–Thou

Part 2 of *The Basic Problems of Phenomenology* is "The Fundamental On-tological Question of the Meaning of Being in General." As mentioned, part 2 has only one rather long chapter: "The Problem of the Ontological Difference." The reason for this single chapter is that Heidegger did not lecture on all the subject matter that he had planned to discuss during the summer semester of 1927. In his introduction to the lectures, he explained that the lecture series would have three parts, with four chapters in each part. The semester ended, however, and he had only covered part 1 and the first chapter of part 2. When Heidegger decided to publish the lecture series as a book, almost five decades after the lectures had been presented, he did not add anything to the text that he had taught in class. The book ends with the single chapter of part 2, which is 149 pages long in German; in this chapter we find Heidegger's first critique of the I–Thou.

The ontological difference mentioned in the title of the chapter refers to the difference between Being and beings. Heidegger again states an idea that he has already repeatedly pronounced: To be able to compre-hend the distinction between Being and beings you must begin by in-vestigating the being of Dasein. His reason is that, among all the beings with whom we are acquainted, only to the ontological constitution of Dasein belongs the understanding of Being. As is evident from his sur-vey of the thinking on Being of philosophers of the past, and as he has shown clearly in the lectures constituting part 1 of the lecture course, Dasein's understanding of Being is very often veiled and obscure. Much of this obscurity occurred, Heidegger believes, because past thinkers did not investigate the ontology of Dasein. Hence, any quest for understanding Being requires that we should endeavor to bring "to light the ground of the basic structures of the Dasein in their unity and wholeness."[1] As in *Being and Time*, Heidegger holds that to illuminate the basic ontological structures of Dasein, we must understand time and temporality. He states clearly that Dasein's ontological constitution is rooted in time and temporality.

In accordance with his usual method of approaching a philosophical problem, Heidegger begins with a historical survey of how thinkers of the past explained time and temporality. He announces that Aristotle's discussion is crucial for any understanding of time. That is probably the reason Heidegger devotes more than twenty pages of this chapter to some of Aristotle's insights. I will not summarize Heidegger's enlightening survey of Aristotle's thinking on time, since it is not crucial to his critique of the I–Thou. Nor do I believe that this survey adds substantially to his fundamental ontology. The survey primarily presents a background for the linking of time to the fundamental ontology of Dasein. Heidegger states his reason for this survey: "Aristotle's definition of time is only the *initial approach* to the interpretation of time."[2]

Following his survey, Heidegger explains that it is mistaken to relate to, or to define, time as if it were a series of "nows." Time emerges, he holds, as primordially linked to Dasein as Being-in-the-world. The fundamental ontology of Dasein should reveal to us the transitoriness of the "now" and the interrelations of past, present, and future in the "now." It should also clarify how time "embraces beings."[3]

Heidegger believes that the way Dasein uses clocks partially illuminates its fundamental ontology and helps to clarify its relation to time. In most instances, when Dasein looks at a clock, it is not concerned with the clock as an object. Dasein primarily looks at a clock in order to discover what the clock shows concerning time. Caution, however, is necessary because, usually when I look at the clock I am not attempting to comprehend the Being of time. I may look at my watch when I wish to gauge how much time is still required for a task in which I am engaged to be finished, say, my cooking of the rabbit stew. I may also consult a clock to check how much time remains before the concert begins. Put differently, I look at the clock in order to reckon with time and to take time into account. And I reckon with time, and take it into account, in order to embark upon or to continue specific engagements.

Thus, when I look at a clock, time has already been unveiled to me. Only on the basis of this prior unveiling can I reckon with time when looking at a clock. In short, Dasein's Being-in-the-world is already an unveiling of time. As Heidegger indicates, Dasein's existing in a world is based upon continually relating to the past, to the present, and to the future; this relating is primary, and on the basis of this relating, Dasein enpresents the "now."

The time that appears on the clock has significance for Dasein; in its everyday Being-in-the-world, Dasein constantly reckons with time and expresses this reckoning in words and deeds. Hence, Heidegger states, significance is one of the structural factors of expressed time. He points to four such structural factors and discusses each factor briefly. A second structural factor, linked to significance, is datability. Dasein is constantly existing the "now" of the present and frequently relating to a specific "now" in the past or in the future; all these "nows" are dated. Every "now" dates itself in relation to certain happenings.

Consider three statements that include an expression of dating: "The first time I wept as an adult was when I heard Beethoven's Ninth Symphony." "As I look into your eyes I sense our deep friendship." "Let us meet next year in Jerusalem for the Pesach Seder." These examples show that you can date a specific "now" without the dating being linked directly to the dates marked on a calendar. Using a calendar is only one particular manner of dating. Thus, time, as expressed and lived by Dasein, is not a freely floating stream of "nows." The structure of every "now" includes datability. When a specific "now" is expressed by Dasein, it is always dated and relates to something in the world.

The third structural factor of expressed time is spannedness. When I say, "Next year in Jerusalem," I am asserting and articulating the spannedness of time from now until next year. When I say, "As I look into your eyes" I am asserting and articulating the spannedness of time during the short period in which my eyes and yours are locked together in a gaze into each other. Heidegger adds, "Every time-moment is spanned intrinsically, the span's breadth being variable."[4]

The fourth structural factor of time is publicness. When we make statements relating to time, or to the "now," such as the statements I gave above, other people will usually understand the statements. Dasein relates to time while Being-with other Daseins, and often in discourse with other Daseins. Time statements are, therefore, usually public knowledge. Heidegger summarizes that the structural factors of time point to the link between time and Dasein's existence.

* * *

Following his presentation of the structural factors of expressed time, Heidegger returns to an idea basic to his thinking. From its structural factors, we can learn that expressed time originates in the ecstatic existential temporality of Dasein. Above, in Chapter 3, I pointed out that, in *Being and Time*, Heidegger asserts that Dasein's ecstatic existence is the origin of its relations to the past, the present, and the future. Heidegger emphasizes this idea when he writes: "Die ekstatisch bestimmt Zeitlichkeit ist die Bedingung der Seinsverfassung des Daseins."[5] I translate this sentence thus: The ecstatically determined temporality is the condition of the constitution of the Being of Dasein. Put differently, Heidegger states that Temporality, with its three ecstases, is the condition for the particular constitution of Dasein's Being.

It is this temporality-conditioned constitution which is unique to Dasein's Being and which differentiates it from all other beings with which we are acquainted. The constitution of a quark, a stone, a tulip, a moth, a cat, a black hole, or a statue by Michelangelo is not temporality-conditioned. None of these beings relate to the world on the basis of the three ecstases. Nor do these beings relate to their environment on the basis of anything resembling an ecstases. Heidegger adds that intentionality, which is basic to Dasein's Being, has the condition of its possibility in the temporality and the ecstases which are unique to Dasein's constitution.

Heidegger's next step is to show that the commonsense understanding of time, as a series of "nows," can be derived from the structural factors of expressed time, and hence from Dasein's Temporality. I will not present his arguments, which seem valid. More important is his question, Why does Dasein view time as an external series of "nows," when the ecstases of time are the condition for the constitution of its own Being? Put differently, if, as Heidegger states, Dasein "is intrinsically temporal in an original fundamental way,"[6] why does Dasein commonly view time as external and extant, as a series of "nows"? Heidegger's answer is that Dasein's viewing of time as extant and external is a result of its falling.

As has been shown in the chapters dedicated to *Being and Time*, Heidegger has articulately described Dasein's falling and its succumbing to the banal and inauthentic mode of existence determined by the "They." As a result of Dasein's falling into inauthenticity, and into a banal existence, and also as an expression of its inauthentic existence, Dasein wrongly determines and relates to its own Being as primarily something extant. This determining of its own Being as something extant leads Dasein to an inauthentic relation to Temporality. Inauthentic Dasein that considers itself something extant, without ecstases and without freedom, decides to view time as an extant series of "nows." Thus, Heidegger states, Dasein's view of time as something extant is created in its own fallen image of itself as something extant.

There is much truth in Heidegger's description of Dasein's inauthentic relationship to time and in his linking it to Dasein's unworthy existence. I must nevertheless again comment that he does not mention those unique moments, say, of creativity, or love, or friendship, in which time is not lived by creative or loving persons as a series of "nows." Put differently, Heidegger's descriptions of the way persons relate to time are enlightening; however, his writings repeatedly convey the impression that a profound aloneness always engulfs and encompasses Dasein, including in its Temporality. The Being of Dasein, whom Heidegger presents primarily as the equipment-oriented being, seems to almost exclude the possibility of any enhancing or euphoric meetings between persons—meetings in which time is, somehow, lived differently.

To be faithful to the theme of this book, I must, once again, emphasize this ontological lack in Heidegger's thinking on time and on Dasein's Being. He describes Dasein's Being-in-the-world as primarily equipment-oriented; in his description, which is very praxis-directed, there is no mention of those enchanting, joyous, blissful moments which persons may experience, say, when in love. This point repeatedly emerges in examining all Heidegger's writings during this period. In these writings, Heidegger never mentions the possible wonderful, albeit rare, moments of human existence in which time is grasped differently. His discussion of Dasein, and his description of its being the source of Temporality, ignore these moments. Nor does he make room for, say, joyous or blissful moments in his discussions of time.

Does not this ontological lack reveal Dasein as condemned to a praxis-directed, equipment-oriented, barren, sordid, and often boring existence? Does not this lack of discussion of blissful moments exclude much wisdom about Dasein's relationship to time and to the world?

To give a very brief example, think of the limited, yet illuminating, wisdom found in the whimsical epitaph the poet Robert Frost proposed for himself: "I had a lover's quarrel with the world."[7] The phrase "a lover's quarrel with the world" seems to not at all fit Heidegger's presentation of Dasein as primarily equipment-oriented and praxis-directed in its Being-in-the-world. Yet, for many readers, myself included, Frost's wry epitaph epitomizes the summary of what can constitute a most worthy mode of existence.

* * *

The first mention of the I–Thou in this chapter appears in the short subsection "Understanding As a Basic Determination of Being-in-the-world." Heidegger opens the general section, to which this subsection belongs, with the statement that he wants to show that Temporality is the condition of the possibility of all understanding of Being. In the subsection, however, he concentrates on clarifying what is understanding. As already stated in previous chapters, Heidegger believes that underlying Dasein's understanding of beings is an understanding of Being, albeit a vague understanding. He supports this statement by reminding us that a major aspect of Dasein's Being is its comporting itself toward beings. Consequently, understanding, as a common manner of Dasein comporting itself toward beings, is an original and basic determination of Dasein's existence. He states: "To exist is essentially, even if not only, to understand."[8] Understanding, Heidegger adds, is central to and crucial for Dasein's attempts to realize its possibilities. And by realizing its possibilities, Dasein expresses its freedom to be this unique person.

Heidegger's description of understanding, as constitutive of Dasein's existence, accords with his continual portrayal of Dasein as primarily equipment-oriented. He states that understanding means Dasein's projecting itself upon a possibility. From a phenomenological perspective, Dasein's projecting of itself includes two things. What Dasein projects itself upon and who is being projected.

A vivid literary example of Heidegger's equipment-oriented description of Dasein's understanding, as projecting itself upon a possibility, is the miser, Monsieur Grandet, the father of Honoré de Balzac's Eugénie Grandet in the novel by that name.[9] Monsieur Grandet fanatically projects himself upon the possibility of constantly enlarging and vigilantly guarding his material wealth, and especially his hoard of gold. Thus we can ask: Who is Monsieur Grandet? The answer emerging from the novel accords with Heidegger's thoughts. Monsieur Grandet is the inauthentic, fallen miser, whose understanding of his own life and of human existence means constantly projecting himself upon the possibility of increasing his wealth. Balzac describes how this understanding determines, informs, and unveils Grandet's daily existence; it also constitutes a crucial component of his greedy, shallow, and inauthentic self-understanding.

As Balzac's novel shows, it is precisely in accordance with this miserly understanding that Grandet temporalizes himself, that is, relates ecstatically to the past, the present, and the future. However, a major conclusion that also emerges from the novel is that Monsieur Grandet is not at all a dialogical person. He never, but never, genuinely shares his thoughts or wishes or beliefs with others; he never relates to other persons as partners in this world. One result of this extreme antidialogical existence is that Grandet is emotionally barren in all his relations with other persons. Furthermore, he does his utmost to strangle all emotions in whomever he encounters, including his wife and his only child, Eugénie. He always perceives other persons, including his wife and daughter, as mere means that will assist him in attaining the goals of his insatiable avarice.

I am not sure that Heidegger would agree with all my conclusions concerning Monsieur Grandet, especially concerning his relations to other persons. Heidegger explains that his presentation of understanding assumes Being-with-others as belonging essentially to Dasein's Being-in-the-world. He indicates that the fundamental ontological state of Dasein is Being-in-the-world, and relations to other persons, or in his terms, relations between Dasein and Dasein, are based on this fundamental state. Thus, Heidegger would hold that sharing with another person means that each partner shares with the Other his or her understanding and Being-in-the-world, which includes recognition of other persons. In this context, he cautions against turning from a solipsism of the ego to "einen Solipsismus zu Zweien im Ich–Du-Verhaltnis"[10]—a solipsism of the dyad in an I–Thou relationship.

Thus, Heidegger's first critique of the I–Thou does not result from an ontological description or an analysis of this relationship. Nor does his first critique of the I–Thou stem from his attempt to relate this relationship to his thinking about Dasein. Rather, in the course of presenting and illuminating the ontology of Dasein's understanding, he merely cautions that the I–Thou is a solipsism of the dyad.

I do not know what a solipsism of the dyad means, and Heidegger does not explain. The phrase "solipsism of the dyad" seems to me to be an oxymoron. I can state categorically, what will be clearly shown in later chapters: it is wrong to define the I–Thou relationship, which Martin Buber described in detail, as any kind of solipsism, including a solipsism of the dyad!

* * *

In the next subsection, Heidegger explains that in all understanding in which Dasein's Being-in-the-world becomes visible and transparent, there is also present an understanding of Being. This statement is important because it reveals, again, that the major direction of Heidegger's thinking is to raise the question of Being. It is therefore correct to conclude that only as an afterthought, or as a corollary to findings that emerge in his continual raising the question of Being, does Heidegger here deal with the ontological status of the I–Thou.

Since understanding is grasped as a projecting by Dasein upon something, Being also can be understood only as it is projected upon something. This statement brings us closer to comprehending Being but also raises many problems which I shall not discuss, such as the relation between Being and time in this projection. Heidegger does point out that Dasein has a preontological understanding of Being, which may partially emerge into the light through the various moods in which Dasein finds itself and through which it frequently discovers its self. This idea accords with his statements on moods, and specifically his discussion of anxiety, in *Being and Time* and in other writings. As in *Being and Time*, here we are again confronted with a tenet basic to Heidegger's fundamental ontology: from an ontological perspective, Dasein's finding its self is a solitary endeavor of its consciousness.

I will not present all the enlightening, subtle, and consequential ideas that Heidegger weaves into his thinking while raising the question of Being. Discussing these ideas in any depth would probably require writing a book. Suffice it to mention that he links the unveiling of Being with knowledge and with the illuminating light of thinking; to support his ideas he returns to Plato's famous parable of the cave in the seventh book of *The Republic*.

Heidegger again briefly mentions the Thou when he responds to the question, How can we describe the link between understanding, which is central to the basic constitution of Dasein, and temporality, in which Dasein is rooted?

In responding to this question, he again points out that *resoluteness* is his term for authentic existence. As explained in *Being and Time*, resoluteness emerges when Dasein chooses to exist and to fulfill its ownmost possibility in face of its own death. In moments of resoluteness, Dasein understands itself from the perspective of its ownmost possibility, death. Put differently, in moments of resoluteness, and in face of its own death, Dasein temporalizes itself as a coming-back-toward-itself from its authentic chosen possibility in the future. Hence, the present of a resolute person is also different from the present of the inauthentic person. The present of a resolute person is not characterized by inauthentic Dasein's equipment-oriented, "They" dominated, thing-engrossed Being-in-the-world. Heidegger calls the authentic present, which emerges when Dasein relates resolutely to its ownmost possibility, the instant. This authentic present emerges in that specific instant which discloses the situation in which Dasein chose to be resolute, and to relate to its future and past resolutely.

On the basis of these major insights concerning Dasein's fundamental ontology, Heidegger again turns to a rejection of the I–Thou. He states that authentic Being-with-one-another determines itself on the basis of individual resoluteness. Here it is important to carefully note Heidegger's language. He does not use words such as *communion, trust, dialogue*, or *good faith* in order to describe an authentic relationship between persons. Indeed, like almost all the instances in which he presents Dasein, his language here is primarily equipment-oriented. The term authentic Being-with-one-another, together with Heidegger's explanation of the term, does not seem to include the generosity and sharing that is revealed in the terms *communion, trust, dialogue*, and *good faith*. To further pursue this point, consider a rather long sentence crucial to Heidegger's ontology of the person.

Being-with-one-another is not a tenacious intrusion of the I upon the thou [sic], derived from their common concealed helplessness; instead, existence as together with one another is founded on the genuine individuation of the individual, determined by enpresenting in the sense of the instant.[11]

Look at this citation, and especially at the locution "common concealed helplessness." The locution reveals a very banal, unthoughtful approach to friendship, love, or genuine dialogue. Genuine friendship is not derived from a joining of helpless people, whose common helplessness is concealed. Genuine friendship requires courage to confront a friend, even while loving him or her. The same is true of love and of genuine dialogue. Suggesting that relations to the Thou are established on a "common concealed helplessness" is, therefore, a stark distortion of marvelous relations that can constitute human reality. It is also a disparaging of Dasein's most enhancing interhuman relations.

Heidegger's major argument in rejecting the I–Thou is found in the second part of the sentence. He states that genuine individuation of the person can only be founded upon resoluteness. He adds to the above sentence the statement that genuine individuation of the person, founded upon resoluteness, is prior to any possible development of the person that arises from dialogue or from the I–Thou relationship.

I believe Heidegger's statement to be very wrong. Among my reasons are the truths that are revealed in Martin Buber's works, especially *I and Thou*. But even before consulting Buber's works, the reader can ponder whether genuine love or friendship is always an outcome of prior individuation of the person, founded upon resoluteness. Is it not closer to truth to hold that genuine love, or dialogue, or friendship are dynamical relations, and, hence, not a necessary outcome of prior individuation? Do not these dynamical relations, whose springing into being is very much a mystery, continually contribute to the personal development and uniqueness—and individuation—of the specific persons involved in the relationship?

Hence, is it not true that, in certain instances, the relations of genuine dialogue, love, and friendship can be prior to what Heidegger calls the individuation of the individual? In summary, can we be totally sure that there is only one track, the track of resoluteness, that leads to individuation of the individual? I suspect that the reader who reflects a bit on these questions will agree that some of Heidegger's ideas on individuation are, at best, problematic, and probably misleading or false.

* * *

In the next subsection, Heidegger quite decisively links Being-in-the-world to his equipment-oriented view of Dasein and to Temporality. As part of his attempts to link Being and time, he discusses the functionality of equipment. He elucidates that, from the perspective of temporality, the context of equipment includes all those beings that Dasein grasps as ready-to-hand. These ready-to-hand beings, which are grasped in their functionality, are crucial for establishing Dasein's Being-in-the-world. He adds that all Dasein's relations with fellow Daseins must be viewed as occurring within the context of Temporality and Being-in-the-world, which are both linked to the functionality of things ready-to-hand.

I disagree. I hold that in his emphatic description of Dasein as equipment-oriented, Heidegger is impoverishing human relations. He is ignoring the many moments of mystery in which a person frequently changes, converts, or enhances his or her existence through intercourse with fellow human beings. Heidegger's position is clear when he states that

Dasein understands itself first and for the most part via things; in unity with that, the co-existence of other Daseins is understood. . . . [B]eing-with others is already implicit in functionality relations.[12]

Thus, these citations reveal that Heidegger views human relations as established primarily on his understanding of Dasein as primarily equipment-oriented. Fortunately, some human relations can be much more profound and worthy than those that are established "via things" and "implicit in functionality relations." These interpersonal relations can be illuminating and may often lead Dasein to reach a deep understanding of itself and of other beings. Hence, I reject the idea that Dasein understands itself first, and for the most part, via the functionality of things.

Based on his presentation of Dasein, Heidegger straightforwardly attacks the I–Thou in a manner that distorts, at least, what Martin Buber wrote. Since this gross distortion reveals much about Heidegger's thinking, I present the German original, followed by my English translation:

Mit dem Ansatz eines Ich–du-Verhaltnis als Verhaltnis zweier Subjekte wäre gesagte, das zunächst zwei Subjekte zu zweien da sind, die sich dann einen Bezug zu anderem verschaffen. Vielmehr, so ursprünglich das Dasein Sein mit Anderen ist, so ursprünglich ist es Sein mit Zuhandenem und Vorhandenem.[13]

With the presentation of an I–Thou relationship as a relationship of two subjects one means, that at first two subjects exist as two, who each then establish a relationship to the other. Rather, just as the original existence of Dasein is with others, its original existence is also with beings ready-to-hand and extant.

Martin Buber would probably agree to the major ideas in the above citation—with some minor qualifications, which I will not elaborate here. I do want to point out Heidegger's distortion of the I–Thou; this distortion occurs because he forgets the I–It.

The first sentences of Buber's *I and Thou* state that the I–Thou does not exist alone, as a primary relationship which overshadows everything else.[14] Rather, as I will soon cite Buber and show, the I–Thou emerges in very unique and rare moments. Usually, a person lives in the realm of the I–It. The I–Thou is extraordinary, and that is what makes it special and worthy. But, from the above citation, we learn that Heidegger sees the I–Thou merely as a relation between two subjects, a relation which emerges like the relation of Dasein to things ready-to-hand. Heidegger does not relate to Buber's distinction between the I–Thou and the I–It, yet he rejects the I–Thou. Such is poor scholarship. Furthermore, the I–Thou that Heidegger mentions, and supposedly refutes, has none of the ontological qualities that Buber's I–Thou includes.

Why does Martin Heidegger, who knew very well how to read texts of philosophers, distort Buber's explicitly stated meaning? I do not know. However, I believe that his distorted manner of presenting the I–Thou can be linked to a fact that has repeatedly emerged in previous chapters. Heidegger describes Dasein as primarily an equipment-oriented and in-authentic being; he did not describe those great moments that can come into being in Daseins's existence—moments that are characterized by genuine love and friendship, or by dialogue, creativity, and generosity. Precisely these moments can make human existence wonderful, worthy, and enhancing. Could it be that these great moments have almost no place in Martin Heidegger's early thinking?

My critique of Heidegger also helps to clarify why he repeatedly re-turned to refuting the I–Thou, in the spirit of the above citation. Thus he writes:

Self and world are not two beings, like subject and object, or like I and thou [sic], but self and world are the basic determination of the Dasein itself in the unity of the structure of being-in-the-world [sic]. Only because the "subject" is deter-mined by being-in-the-world [sic] can it become as this self a thou [sic] for an-other.[15]

Thus, the above citation suggests that like the terms *self* and *world*, which, he holds, are not two beings, the I–Thou creates problems for Heideg-ger's fundamental ontology. Yet, instead of relating to this problem as an opportunity for reaching a profounder and broader understanding of Dasein's existence, Heidegger's text endeavors to eradicate the mystery of the I–Thou. He overlooks the fact that with such an eradication much of the glory of being human vanishes.

It is, therefore, appropriate to again state categorically: Dasein is not only a tool-using and thinking being; there are aspects of being human, such as love, dialogue, generosity, and creativity that exist and whose coming into being are mysteries. By ignoring these aspects of Dasein's Being-in-the-world in his early thinking, Heidegger eradicates much of Dasein's stature and glory. In the process, he also diminishes Dasein's Being.

Put succinctly, Heidegger's rejection and dismissal of the I–Thou has unfortunate implications for his fundamental ontology. Together with the discarding of the I-Thou, and the ignoring of other worthy human relations, Heidegger wrongly endeavors to establish the nonmysterious remnant of human relations as the only basis of his fundamental ontology. The everyday Dasein that he presents is primarily equipment-oriented, determined by the "They," and inauthentic. Indeed, Heidegger's Dasein is a rather banal, quite boring being who seems to be capable of being resolute and of thinking authentically only when facing its own death. Love and dialogue, creativity, courage, and generosity are never primary and seem to be remote possibilities in the everyday Dasein that he presents. Also, the pursuit of justice seems to be far beyond Dasein's comprehension. Consequently, it seems quite evident that Buber's I-Thou relationship interferes with Heidegger's ideas on what constitutes a fundamental ontology.

At this point, I can already venture to state a sad conclusion. In his stubborn rejection of the I-Thou—as an important aspect of Dasein's existence and its Being-in-the-world—Heidegger is narrowing and diminishing the horizon of the fundamental ontology of Dasein that he has painstakingly presented.

* * *

In the final pages of this chapter, which are also the final pages of *The Basic Problems of Phenomenology*, Heidegger links his presentation of Dasein and of Being to temporality. Although one may find valuable insights in these pages, the theme of his thinking is not linked directly to the ontological status of the I-Thou. To continue my description and evaluation of Heidegger's critique of the I-Thou, and its relation to his fundamental ontology, I turn to his series of lectures presented at the University of Marburg in the winter semester of 1928.

NOTES

1. Martin Heidegger, *The Basic Problems of Phenomenology*, trans. Albert Hofstadter (Bloomington: Indiana University Press, 1982), p. 227.

2. Ibid., p. 257.

3. Ibid.

4. Ibid., p. 264.

5. Martin Heidegger, *Die Grundprobleme der Phänomenologie* (Frankfurt am Main: Vittorio Klostermann, 1975), p. 378.

6. Heidegger, *Basic Problems*, p. 271.

7. *The Poetry of Robert Frost*, ed. Edward Connery Lathem (New York: Holt, Rinehart and Winston, 1969), p. 355.

8. Heidegger, *Basic Problems*, p. 276.

9. Honoré de Balzac, *Eugénie Grandet*, trans. Marion Anton Crawford (Middlesex, Eng.: Penguin, 1955).

10. Heidegger, *Grundprobleme*, p. 394.

11. Heidegger, *Basic Problems*, p. 288.

12. Ibid., p. 296.

13. Heidegger, *Grundprobleme*, p. 421.

14. Martin Buber, *I and Thou*, trans. Ronald Gregor Smith (New York: Scribner's, 1958), p. 3.

15. Heidegger, *Basic Problems*, p. 297.

Chapter 6

The I–Thou in Heidegger's Study of Kant

Heidegger's book *Phenomenological Interpretation of Kant's "Critique of Pure Reason"*[1] is based on his lectures in the course that he taught during the 1928 winter semester at the University of Marburg. The lectures were first published as a book in 1977, after Heidegger's death. However, much of the thinking presented in these lectures was published in 1929, in Heidegger's book *Kant and the Problem of Metaphysics*.[2] In the preface, Heidegger noted that many of the ideas presented in this book were developed and thought out in the lecture course given at the winter semester of 1928 at the University of Marburg.

In *Kant and the Problem of Metaphysics*, Heidegger criticizes many approaches relating to Kant's thought presented by the neo-Kantians, whose thinking was very influential in Germany in the late nineteenth century and the early twentieth century. Although the two books often deal with the same problems, *Phenomenological Interpretation of Kant's "Critique of Pure Reason"* is not identical with *Kant and the Problem of Metaphysics*. For instance, two brief critiques of the I–Thou are found in the book based on the lectures. There is no mention of the I–Thou in *Kant and the Problem of Metaphysics*.

Heidegger's two books on Kant have been recognized by some thinkers as important contributions to Kantian scholarship. The books suggest that you can find in the *Critique of Pure Reason* many important ontological truths that have been overlooked for many decades. Most important, these ontological truths reject, at least partially, the prevailing interpretation of Kant's writings adopted by the neo-Kantians, by many

twentieth-century analytic philosophers, and by many epistemologists—
all of whom viewed Kant's thinking primarily as a major contribution
to epistemology. According to Heidegger, Kant's main contribution is in
helping to clear the way and to indicate the basis for a fundamental
ontology. These views, as may be expected, aroused much criticism and
also disputation. One recorded response is found in the second appendix
of *Kant and the Problem of Metaphysics*, which is titled "Davos Disputation
between Ernst Cassirer and Martin Heidegger." In this published disputation Ernst Cassirer, a leading neo-Kantian philosopher, and Martin
Heidegger attempt to elucidate to each other the areas and the foundation of their disagreement concerning the interpretation of Kant's thinking, especially the *Critique of Pure Reason*.

In their recorded disputation, Cassirer and Heidegger seem to be
wanting to learn from each other. However, not all critiques of Heidegger's interpretation of Kant were amicable. In the preface to the second
edition of *Kant and the Problem of Metaphysics*, which was published in
1950, Heidegger writes, "Readers have taken constant offence at the violence of my interpretations. Their allegation of violence can indeed be
supported by this text."[3] To justify himself, he asserts that any thoughtful
dialogue between thinkers upon crucial philosophical problems will always be correctly subjected to the charge of violence of interpretations.
I do not agree with this assertion but will not challenge it here.

The interpretation of Kant's *Critique of Pure Reason* that Heidegger
presents in these two books has little relevance to the theme of my study.
Hence I will not make any attempt to summarize it. Nor will I attempt
to evaluate the validity of his interpretations of Kant's thinking. My impression is that during this period of his thinking, Heidegger studied
Kant's philosophy and interpreted it mainly in order to find support, in
the thinking of this great philosopher, for some of his own ideas on Being
and on time. By interpreting Kant's *Critique of Pure Reason*, he seemed to
believe that he could show the significance of the fundamental ontology
presented in *Being and Time*. Here is one brief example.

A major thrust of Heidegger's lecture course and of the ideas found
in *Kant and the Problem of Metaphysics* is to prove the centrality of time,
both for human existence and for any thoughtful response to the question of Being. Consider, for instance, two sentences from the two opening
paragraphs of the last, summarizing section of *Kant and the Problem of
Metaphysics*.

Kant's laying of the ground for metaphysics, as unprecedented resolute questioning about the inner possibility of the manifestness of the Being of beings
must come up against time as the basic determination of finite transcendence, if
in fact the understanding of Being in Dasein projects Being from itself upon time,
so to speak.

It is not because time functions as a "form of intuition" and was interpreted as such at the point of entry into the *Critique of Pure Reason*, but because the understanding of Being must be projected upon time from out of the ground of the finitude of Dasein in man, that time, in essential unity with the transcendental power of imagination, attained the central metaphysical function in the *Critique of Pure Reason*.[4]

This citation indicates that by showing and holding that Kant's thinking points to the ontological significance of time, Heidegger musters support for his own thoughts on the centrality of time for our understanding of the Being of Dasein. As I have shown, such thoughts were central to the ontology presented in *Being and Time*. Put differently, Heidegger's interpretation of Kant's *Critique of Pure Reason* is often based on, and directed toward, his own concepts and the fundamental ontology that he has presented. I want to again mention that Heidegger's interpretations of Kant's thinking that support his summary are not important for the theme of this book.

It is, however, important to note that Kant's writings, very much like Heidegger's books and essays, give very little space and thought to interhuman relations—say, to friendship and love. I can state categorically: The ontology of interhuman relations is not discussed in depth in the many writings of these two seminal thinkers. We should, therefore, not be surprised that Heidegger sought, and believed that he had found, support for his fundamental ontology in Kant's writings.

* * *

Heidegger's first mention of the I–Thou in *Phenomenological Interpretation of Kant's "Critique of Pure Reason"* is included in his brief discussion of Being-in-the-world, a discussion which adds nothing to what was presented on this important theme in *Being and Time*. In this context, he writes two sentences that are hardly enlightening:

"World" is that particular whole toward which we comport ourselves at all times. The personal relation of one existence to another is also not a free floating cognitive relation of an I-self to a thou-self, as if they were isolated souls; but rather each is a factical self in a world, and the being of the self is essentially determined by its comportment to the world.[5]

There is something ignoble and inane about this brief citation. It would be very difficult to find a respected thinker who defines or discusses interhuman relations as "a free floating cognitive relation of an I-self to a thou-self." Therefore, I wonder: Who is Heidegger criticizing and attacking?

All the thinkers who discuss the ontology of interhuman relations whose writings I have read—Plato, Cicero, Søren Kierkegaard, Buber,

Nikolay Berdyaev, Gabriel Marcel, and others—understand and state explicitly that persons exist in a world. They may not agree with Heidegger's formulations on what constitutes a world, but they definitely do not view relations between persons as "free floating cognitive" relations. Many of these thinkers also state categorically that persons relate to each other within a situation that includes their personal history and also the history and the everyday facts of the world. Put differently, these thinkers emphasize that a person relates to other persons in specific situations that emerge in the world.

Why does Heidegger, who read extensively, suggest that there are thinkers who hold that human relations are "a free floating cognitive relation of an I-self to a thou-self"? Why does he present and attempt to criticize such a caricature of human relations? Why does he need to support his enlightening, valid, and important thoughts on Being-in-the-world by presenting such a misinformed statement concerning human relations?—I do not know.

Perhaps Heidegger felt that in *Being and Time* he had not given the ontology of interhuman relations sufficient thought, and, therefore, he wanted to dismiss interhuman relations as irrelevant to his major findings. Such an approach would be unfortunate. Before abandoning Heidegger's inane observation, however, I should add that, according to Martin Buber, the I–Thou relationship always occurs within the world.

* * *

The second instance in which Heidegger mentions the I–Thou reveals much about his understanding—or misunderstanding—of this relationship. Here is the entire paragraph in which his critique of the I–Thou appears. It appears toward the end of the book.

> The emphasis placed on the original transcendence of Dasein is also significant for Kant's practical philosophy. Only because Dasein can be with itself on the basis of transcendence can Dasein be with another self as a thou [*Du*] in the world. The I–thou relation is not itself already the relation of transcendence. Rather the I–thou relation is grounded in the transcendence of Dasein. It is a mistake to assume that the I–thou relation as such primarily constitutes the possible discovery of the world. This relation may just make the discovery of the world impossible. For example, the I–thou relation of *ressentiment* may hinder me from seeing the world of the other. The much discussed psychological and psychoanalytical problems of the I–thou relation are without philosophical foundation if they are not grounded in the fundamental ontology of Dasein.[6]

Ignore, for a moment, the defensive ontological statements in this citation. One unfortunate truth immediately emerges: Heidegger attacked the I–Thou without carefully reading Buber's *I and Thou*. If Heidegger had read *I and Thou* carefully, he never would have written the phrase "the I–thou relation of *ressentiment*." As will emerge clearly in the chapters dedicated to Buber's presentation of the I–Thou, *ressentiment* can never—but never—be an I–Thou relation. Hence, Heidegger's phrase reveals, at best, irresponsible scholarship. More likely, it reveals a total lack of understanding of what the I–Thou relation and a life of genuine dialogue are all about.

In the citation, Heidegger rejects the I–Thou in the context of his discussion of transcendence. His basic thinking on intentionality and transcendence was presented above, in Chapter 4. Here he formulates his position a bit differently. In the paragraph that precedes the above citation, he criticizes Kant for not seeing that transcendence is the "essential determination of the ontological constitution of Dasein."[7] As we learn from the citation, Heidegger's next step is to hold that Dasein's being with itself is ontologically prior to its being with other Daseins. How does he determine this priority? He does not explain. Thus, even if we accept Heidegger's statement concerning transcendence as the essential determination of the ontological constitution of Dasein, the statement does not prove that Dasein's Being-with itself is prior to its Being-with other Daseins.

Let us briefly examine this point. Could it not be possible to state the opposite of what Heidegger states? Consider the statement: Only because Dasein can be with another self as a Thou in the world can Dasein be with itself on the basis of transcendence. Is this statement totally farfetched? I think not. Furthermore, I would argue that this statement is tenable on the basis of Heidegger's presentation of Dasein as thrown and as Being-in-the-world. I also would hold that the statement accords with the idea that transcendence is the essential determination of the ontological constitution of Dasein.

Dasein relates transcendentally as a Being-in-the-world to beings that it meets and encounters. Among these beings are other persons. I assume that for most Daseins, these other persons are the most significant among the many beings whom they may meet. The reason for this preference is clear. Only with other persons can Dasein speak and have verbal intercourse. Only with other persons can Dasein share its thoughts, feelings, and concerns. Only together with other persons can Dasein share truths that have been unconcealed.

Consider the centrality of language in the interhuman relationships that Dasein establishes. Different languages belong to different groups of Daseins who live together and establish a world. Speaking and having verbal intercourse are of the essence of being human and are crucial to being able to establish a world. One of the reasons animals live in an environment and not in a world is that animals cannot speak. Consequently, animals do not partake in living with language with which Dasein establishes a world. I would add that Heidegger never emphasized this point sufficiently during this period of his thought.

Only because Dasein exists with other persons can Dasein live within a language and establish all those relations that are based on language and on verbal intercourse. These relations are crucial for establishing a world and for Dasein as Being-in-the-world. I would further hold that Dasein can be with itself on the basis of transcendence only because Dasein can speak and hear other persons who also speak, hear, and understand speech—and speak a specific language, be it Chinese, Arabic, Portuguese, or Greek. Put differently, Dasein can be with itself on the basis of transcendence only because it is a being who can conduct and participate in verbal intercourse with other Daseins, only because it exists within a specific language and is a being who daily uses language. Before Dasein can speak and understand a language, before Dasein can relate to others and to oneself with the help of language, it is very doubtful, that Dasein could recognize a personal self—neither its own self nor a self of an Other. Consequently, Dasein, as Being-in-the-world, is Dasein who shares a language with other Daseins. A simple example of the crucial role that language plays is that one of the ways of recognizing a person is by that person's name, which requires that both those who recognize the person and the person recognized exist within and use a specific language.

The gist of this brief look at language is that even if we accept some of Heidegger's ontological assumptions concerning Dasein, they do not necessarily lead to his statement that Dasein's being with itself is primary. Consequently, his major rejection of the I–Thou in the above citation—that it is not primary and not a relation of transcendence—is not proven.

Concerning the I–Thou, one additional comment is appropriate. This comment is based on my personal living through I–Thou encounters and on similar experiences described by other persons. As intimated earlier, I have also found descriptions of I–Thou encounters in great literature. These findings have taught me that we must always remember the primacy of language for interhuman relations.

As a language-speaking being, from early childhood Dasein persistently intermingles with other language-speaking beings. Among these others may be a person whom Dasein has encountered, could encounter, or will encounter as a Thou. When such an I–Thou encounter occurs, when persons realize that they have lived through such a moment of grace, both participants in the encounter recognize that the moment of the encounter was primal and that it transcended time. Hence, in the above citation, Heidegger wrongly rejects a primary human encounter that exists and that has been documented in biographies and in literature. Certainly, he did not give the I–Thou encounter due recognition and thought.

These findings lead me to conclude that Heidegger's criticism and rejection of the I–Thou in his book *Phenomenological Interpretation of Kant's "Critique of Pure Reason"* is wrong. The criticism is based on a fundamental misunderstanding of the I–Thou. The rejection is supported by unproven and unconvincing statements that, Heidegger believes, stem from his own ontology.

NOTES

1. Martin Heidegger, *Phenomenological Interpretation of Kant's "Critique of Pure Reason,"* trans. Parvis Emad and Kenneth Maly (Bloomington: Indiana University Press, 1997).

2. Martin Heidegger, *Kant and the Problem of Metaphysics*, trans. Richard Taft (Bloomington: Indiana University Press, 1990).

3. Ibid., p. xviii.

4. Ibid., p. 166.

5. Heidegger, *Phenomenological Interpretation*, p. 14.

6. Ibid., p. 214.

7. Ibid., p. 213.

Chapter 7

Metaphysics and Logic

The last lecture course that Heidegger gave at the University of Marburg, before moving to the University of Freiburg—with which he was affiliated for the remainder of his academic career—was in the summer semester of 1928. The book *The Metaphysical Foundations of Logic*, first published in 1978, three years after Heidegger's death, is based on the manuscript that Heidegger prepared for this lecture course and on the notes of the lectures taken by two former students.[1] The first part of the book is primarily a presentation and an interpretation of Leibnitz's ideas on thinking and on logic, including his views on monads and on the foundations of logic. In the second part of the book, Heidegger discusses what he calls the metaphysical foundations of logic.

Heidegger's thoughts on the metaphysical foundations of logic are intertwined with the major themes of his thinking during this period. Thus, the second half of the book discusses at some length both Being and time as linked to the foundations of logic. In this discussion, he returns to concepts and to ideas presented in *Being and Time*; he also discusses themes brought up in the other lecture courses that he gave at the University of Marburg, which have been the topics of the last three chapters. Of course, as his thought develops, Heidegger frequently views these major themes of his thinking from a somewhat different perspective. In *The Metaphysical Foundations of Logic*, he adds depth and breadth to his previous thoughts by relating his own ideas to the thinking of Leibnitz and, of course, to the metaphysical foundations of logic.

In the second part of the book Heidegger also presents his most forceful and definitive rejection of the I–Thou. He endeavors to reject the primary ontological status of the I–Thou. He dedicates a few pages to explaining and justifying this rejection. In this chapter, I shall not describe Heidegger's elucidation of Leibnitz's thinking, nor his thinking on and his presentation of the metaphysical foundations of logic. I do not believe that these topics add substantially to his fundamental ontology, which I briefly outlined in previous chapters. I will concentrate on Heidegger's definitive rejection of the I–Thou and on how this rejection is linked to his fundamental ontology.

* * *

Heidegger discusses the I–Thou in chapter 11 of *The Metaphysical Foundations of Logic*, which is called "Transcendence of Dasein," in the section of the chapter titled "Freedom and World." In this section he wants to, at least partially, elucidate the relationship between the freedom of Dasein and what he calls the primary character of the world which Dasein establishes, and is engaged in, as Being-in-the-world. Heidegger calls this primary character of the world a for-the-sake-of-which; it is a term for the purposiveness of Dasein, which is the being who establishes and engages in a world.

Heidegger holds that, as a whole being, Dasein constantly transcends whatever meets it—be it a person or an object—toward a world which is primarily defined as its for-the-sake-of-which. He concedes that Dasein's constant transcending toward a world may bring up a question: what is the purpose, the for-the-sake-of, for which humans exist? Heidegger states categorically that there is no general or objective answer to this question. Rather, each person alone, who questions Being and beings, can pose the question of his or her purpose, of his or her for-the-sake-of-which, and, perhaps, answer it.

To better comprehend Dasein's response to the question of the for-the-sake-of-which, Heidegger distinguishes between truths that have to do with extant beings and truths about what exists. He explains that questions and truths about what exists include, during the act of questioning, the situation of the questioner. In Shakespeare's play *Romeo and Juliet*, when Romeo asks Juliet if she loves him, he does not ask about an extant being. Rather, Romeo questions Juliet about a truth that, perhaps, exists as part of, and greatly influences, her Being-in-the-world. Romeo's own situation, his Being-in-the-world, is included in the questioning. Indeed, Shakespeare's sad tragedy clearly shows that Romeo questions Juliet from within a dire social situation in Verona, a situation which daily influences his life. It is also evident that Romeo's questioning of Juliet concerning her love for him is linked to the purpose of his existence, to his for-the-sake-of-which.

Heidegger rejects the attacks made on his thinking that, because of his emphasis on the centrality of the for-the-sake-of-which in Dasein's existence, he is proposing an extreme egotism. I agree with his rejection, and I believe that the example of Romeo and Juliet firmly supports Heidegger's statement. An extreme egotist cannot love as Romeo loved, and Romeo's existence and decisions pretty well fit Heidegger's presentation of the for-the-sake-of-which.

However, I begin to question the truth of Heidegger's ideas when he states that, with the help of the for-the-sake-of-which, he presented an ontological metaphysical description of egoicity, and of Dasein. Furthermore, I disagree when he writes that this description of egoicity fits Dasein's primary determination, hence it also determines the status of the I–Thou:

Only because Dasein is primarily determined by egoicity can it factically exist as a thou for and with another Dasein. The thou is not an ontical replicate of a factical ego; but neither can a thou exist as such and be itself a thou for another ego if it is not at all Dasein, i.e., if it is not grounded in egoicity. The egoicity belonging to the transcendence of Dasein is the metaphysical condition of the possibility for a thou to be able to exist and for an I–thou relationship to be able to exist.[2]

Heidegger here states that egoicity precedes all relationships with other persons. Two basic questions emerging from this citation are, What does Heidegger's term *egoicity* mean? What does egoicity encompass? A bit further in his explanation he states that, in the selfhood of the I, egoicity is identical with freedom. But again, this statement reveals very little about egoicity. What is more, if such an identity exists, what need do we have of the term *egoicity*?

To show the lack of clarity in the above citation, and in Heidegger's accompanying explanation, you can merely replace the term *egoicity* with the term *freedom* in the citation. One result would be following sentence: "The freedom belonging to the transcendence of Dasein is the metaphysical condition of the possibility for a thou to be able to exist and for an I–thou relationship to be able to exist." This sentence, however, is trivial; it teaches nothing. No thinker whom I have read would challenge the idea that the freedom belonging to the transcendence of a person is necessary for an I–Thou relationship to come into being.

The problem that Heidegger seems to have ignored is that the ego, or the I, is a very complex being; it evades clear-cut descriptions or reductions to a simple formula. Heidegger's definition and presentation of egoicity, as based on his own terms, including the above citation, skims over much of this complexity. His definition attempts to reduce the ego in a manner that would fit his ontology of Dasein. But such a definition and such a reduction impoverish the ego and hardly enlighten us. Much the same is true of Heidegger's emphasis on the for-the-sake-of-which. As with the term *egoicity*, you can ask again: If the for-the-sake-of-which is understood merely as an expression of freedom, what need do we have of this cumbersome Heideggerian term?

Furthermore, in the above citation Heidegger does not describe the ego or egoicity; he merely states his position concerning the I–Thou without proving or establishing that it is correct. Nor does he present examples from life that support his position concerning the I–Thou or any of his other statements. Without a description of the ego and without any examples from life that would support his unproven statements, Heidegger's presentation is very problematic.

To partially illuminate these problems, I return, for a moment, to an approach that I adopted in Chapter 6 and ask the following question. Is there not a possibility of holding that the opposite of Heidegger's statement is true? Consider the following statement, which is the opposite of what Heidegger states in the last sentence of the above citation: Only because Dasein can factically exist as a Thou for and with another Dasein, will it be determined as an ego and acquire egoicity. I do not think that this statement, which Buber would probably have supported, is absurd. Nor do I think that Heidegger has presented an ontological foundation, or any other evidence, which can invalidate the opposite of what he believes.

* * *

Why did Heidegger present such problematic statements as those cited above? Recall that Heidegger's fundamental ontology and his metaphysical thinking, together with his raising of the question of Being, begin with an attempt to comprehend the being of Dasein. As he presents Dasein, however, its unique being, which is thrown into the world, precedes and is fundamental to all its human relations. This presentation of Dasein is metaphysical and not existential. It is not supported by examples or by supportive descriptions from Dasein's life. Moreover, in the context of his rejection of the I–Thou and, to the best of my knowledge in his other writings, Heidegger never proves that this metaphysical presentation of Dasein is primary. Nor does Heidegger allow for the emergence of any challenge to his conception of Dasein.

Despite these quite evident drawbacks, Heidegger believes that his metaphysical presentation of Dasein is true; moreover, he believes it to be sound enough to reduce all human relations and all existential findings to such a presentation. He repeatedly indicates that existential findings are secondary to his metaphysical description and to the metaphysical questions that arise from his description. Some of the problems stemming from this, rather dogmatic, approach have been pointed out briefly in previous chapters. Here are a few additional problems.

Relying on his approach that existential findings are secondary to metaphysical descriptions, Heidegger states emphatically that the analysis or the description of the I–Thou cannot solve the metaphysical problems of Dasein, because it cannot even pose these problems. Put differently, the metaphysical problems of Dasein are beyond specific existential encounters and pretty much uninfluenced by them. These problems can only be approached if we view Dasein's selfhood as metaphysically isolated. Heidegger explains:

Pure selfhood, understood as the metaphysical neutrality of Dasein, expresses, at the same time, the metaphysical isolation of Dasein in ontology, an isolation which should never be confused with an egoistic-solipsistic exaggeration of one's own individuality.[3]

Thus, Heidegger emphasizes in this citation the metaphysical isolation of Dasein and views this isolation as being expressed by pure selfhood. It is quite fascinating to recall that a pure unbridgeable metaphysical isolation also characterizes the monads that Leibnitz described, and that these isolated monads are central to Leibnitz's metaphysics and ontology. Heidegger discusses Leibnitzian monads earlier in this book. It is fair to ask, Did the metaphysics in Leibnitz's monadology have any influence on Heidegger's above statements?

In the above citation, however, Heidegger merely points to the metaphysical isolation of Dasein and immediately rejects an "egoistic-solipsistic" exaggeration of individuality as an existential expression of this isolation. Heidegger does not explain in detail what he means by the metaphysical isolation of Dasein; nor does he explain why this isolation can be distorted so as to become an egoistic-solipsistic exaggeration. We can, however, learn a bit about Dasein's metaphysical isolation from his statements that relate to Dasein's Being-with other Daseins.

Many times, even ad nauseam, we pointed out that this being qua Dasein is always already with others and always already with beings not of Dasein's nature. . . . In choosing itself Dasein really chooses precisely its being-with others and precisely its being among beings of a different character. . . . Only because Dasein can expressly choose itself on the basis of its selfhood can it be committed to others. And only because, in being toward itself as such, Dasein can understand anything like a "self" can it furthermore attend at all to a thou-self. Only because, Dasein constituted by the for-the-sake-of, exists in selfhood, only for this reason is anything like human community possible.[4]

It is true that Heidegger frequently pointed out that Dasein as Being-in-the-world is always already with other Daseins and with other beings. Yet in his writings on this topic, he describes the other live persons, with whom Dasein finds itself in the world, and with whom Dasein daily interacts, as rather passive and quite inconsequential. In Heidegger's writings, these other Daseins, these supposedly live active persons whom Dasein encounters every day, seem to have wooden legs; they have no spirit or soul. Their freedom hardly emerges as being able to influence, inspire, or, at times, oppress or enslave Dasein. Consequently, these other persons seem to have minor influence on Dasein's existence.

For example, as already pointed out, in Heidegger's writings I have not found mention of a genuine or an authentic meeting between two or more Daseins. This point is crucial and worth repeating. In the Heidegger corpus, genuine meetings between Daseins, and the exciting possibilities emerging from such meetings, seem to have no primary or lasting relation to Dasein's selfhood. Put differently, in his writings, there is no mention of the influence that genuine meetings may have on Dasein's Being. Dasein's choosing of itself on the basis of its metaphysically isolated pure selfhood is primary.

To see the problems of this way of grasping the selfhood of Dasein, look again at Shakespeare's Romeo and Juliet. Romeo falls in love with Juliet, and she falls in love with Romeo. What does the term "fall in love" mean?

If we accept everyday language, we understand immediately that when Romeo falls in love with Juliet his entire Being is involved in loving Juliet. The same is true of Juliet's falling in love with Romeo. Furthermore, both Romeo and Juliet are each active and passive in this deeply moving engagement of falling in love; for love to exist, the lover must act, but falling is something that happens to a person. The term *falling* expresses this passivity; it expresses the fact that powers, seemingly stronger than Romeo or than Juliet, participate in determining their choices. Thus falling in love often surprises the persons involved. They definitely did not plan it.

Moreover, falling in love, meeting the beloved, is a joyous event that brings great joy to the lover. It very often illuminates the lover's entire Being. As Romeo states when he goes to meet Juliet after consulting with Friar Lawrence, "a joy past joy calls out to me" (act 3, scene 3). Hence, even without giving a full answer to what the term "falls in love" means, it is evident that the term "falls in love" points to a unique singular event, to the possibility of a joyous genuine meeting between the persons involved in loving each other. The possibility of such a unique yet well-documented event of lovers meeting each other, and its ontological significance, is not discussed in Heidegger's writings. Nor does the possibility of such wonderful surprises as "falling in love," accord with Heidegger's understanding of Dasein's metaphysical isolation.

The example of Romeo's love for Juliet leads to two significant questions concerning Heidegger's assertions. First, can we distinguish between Romeo's falling in love with Juliet and his choosing himself on the basis of his selfhood? I do not believe that such a distinction is on-tologically valid. Romeo, as a Dasein thrown into the world, does not choose a specific selfhood that requires or necessitates that he fall in love with Juliet. Rather, in the first meeting between Romeo and Juliet, there is a surprising moment of mystery and of grace, a moment which no person, including the participants, can expect or foretell, a moment in which the participants' passion, spontaneity, love, and freedom emerge. This meeting profoundly influences the being of the participants: Romeo and Juliet fall in love with each other.

We cannot analyze and cannot fully describe such surprising moments of mystery or grace, although we can point to them. Assisted by Hei-degger's later thinking on the significance of poetry for human existence, I have shown, in a recent book, that some poets and writers can illu-minate and disclose the truth of these enhancing moments.[5] But we non-poets can describe only the facts that are in the background of any such genuine meeting. All we can say is something like the following: Romeo meets Juliet and falls in love with her, and she falls in love with him. Shakespeare also shows—in contrast to what Heidegger wrote in the above citation—that this mutual falling in love, this moment of surprise, mystery, love, and grace, contributes to determining both Juliet's self-hood and Romeo's selfhood.

The second question is, Could not someone suggest, in contrast to Heidegger's position, that Romeo's falling in love with Juliet is crucial to his choosing of himself, much as Juliet's falling in love with Romeo is crucial to her choosing of herself? I firmly believe that falling in love is, indeed, crucial to a person's choice of his or her selfhood. Without falling in love with Juliet, it is evident that Romeo's choice of selfhood would be very different. The same is true of Juliet's falling in love with Romeo and her choice of her selfhood.

It seem quite evident, however, that Heidegger would have to disagree with these conclusions. He would have to argue that the metaphysical isolation of Dasein, and the choice of its selfhood, in this case of the choice of selfhood of Romeo or of Juliet, precedes their falling in love with each other. By such an argument, Heidegger would be true to his presentation of Dasein as metaphysically isolated. He would also be true to his repeated rejection of the I–Thou, and to his ignoring of genuine meetings as having any major ontological significance in determining Dasein's Being-in-the-world.

In such arguments, Heidegger would be faithful to his thinking; but he would be dead wrong.

* * *

The metaphysical isolation of Dasein that Heidegger mentioned is now somewhat clearer. If we exclude from the Being of Dasein the possible

ontological priority of genuine meetings between Daseins, which includes the possibility of falling in love, Dasein is ontologically immersed
in a deep metaphysical and existential isolation. But on what grounds
did Heidegger decide that metaphysical and existential isolation have
priority over genuine meetings? I do not know.

What is more, life and great art reject the metaphysical isolation of
Dasein that Heidegger emphasizes. I have already indicated how and
where Shakespeare's play, *Romeo and Juliet*, belies the determined finality
of the metaphysical and existential isolation of Dasein that Heidegger
presents. It is well-nigh impossible to imagine that a person who is metaphysically isolated, whose existence resembles those paragons of metaphysical isolation, the Leibnitzian monads—it is hard to imagine such a
metaphysically isolated person announcing, as Romeo did when hasten-
ing to a meeting with his beloved Juliet, that "a joy past joy calls out to
me." Monads do not meet; nor does it seem that a metaphysically isolated being can experience joy at meeting another metaphysically isolated being. I can only conclude that Dasein's metaphysical isolation,
which Heidegger proclaims to be its ontological fate, is *not* its fate. Metaphysical isolation is merely one of many existential and ontological possibilities that Dasein can choose to live as Being-in-the-world.

Thus, Heidegger's mistake is not that he does not mention Dasein's
Being-with other Daseins. He frequently does mention it. His mistake is
that he never presents the richness, the depth, the sadness, the joy, and
the complexity that can be present, and that can enhance a person's being, in Dasein's Being-with other Daseins. These wonderful moments of
sharing between persons are all ontological possibilities that influence
Dasein's Being. As already mentioned, I do not recall Heidegger ever
discussing, in any detail, the wonderful moments of intimacy, mystery,
and grace that can emerge in a worthy friendship and in genuine meetings between persons. Such moments are not merely social or psychological events or outcomes; they have ontological status. And they are
different from, and not necessarily linked to, falling in love.

Here is a description of a genuine meeting, described by Bertrand Russell, which includes intimacy, mystery, and grace. The meeting led to
the establishing of a genuine friendship between Russell and Joseph Conrad. Note that the meeting transcends any psychological, sociological, or
even metaphysical explanation. I should add that Bertrand Russell was
certainly not an existentialist philosopher. Yet in his book *Portraits from
Memory and Other Essays*, Russell describes his first meeting with the
author Joseph Conrad in terms which accord with the Buberian locution
"genuine meeting."

At our very first meeting, we talked with continually increasing intimacy. We
seemed to sink through layer after layer of what was superficial, till gradually

both reached the central fire. It was an experience unlike any other that I have known. We looked into each other's eyes, half appalled and half intoxicated to find ourselves in such a region. The emotion was as intense as passionate love, and at the same time all embracing. I came away bewildered, and hardly able to find my way among ordinary affairs.[6]

Russell relates that he and Conrad continued to meet, but not frequently; yet all their meetings were genuine and touched the "central fire" of their being.

In Heidegger's detailed descriptions of Dasein, I have not found any mention of the possibility of genuine meetings between two persons such as described by Russell in the citation. I concede that Russell's meeting with Conrad is exceptional, but such meetings exist. I could bring a dozen descriptions of similar meetings from literature—for instance, read the first meeting between Dimitri and Alyosha in Fyodor Dostoyevsky's *The Brothers Karamazov*. Furthermore, Heidegger's persistent ignoring of the significance of the I–Thou, especially as elucidated in Buber's writings on the I–Thou, are additional testimony to the fact that he did not find place in his ontology for genuine meetings.

I can therefore conclude that in his detailed rejection of the I–Thou Heidegger is very wrong. I would also hold that his sweeping conclusion concerning the metaphysical isolation of Dasein is grounded or established on a limited, and hence somewhat distorted, fundamental ontology of Dasein's relations to other Daseins. Let me say it again. Heidegger's emphasis on Dasein's metaphysical isolation is constructed on the seeping bog of his mistaken comprehension of Dasein's manner of Being-with other Daseins.

* * *

To recapitulate, *The Metaphysical Foundations of Logic* is the last publication, that I know of, in which Heidegger publicly rejects the I–Thou. This book does not add any substantial thinking or relevant ideas to his previous shallow rejections. On the other hand, his somewhat detailed discussion of the reasons that he rejects the I–Thou reveals grave limitations in his fundamental ontology of Dasein's Being-with. To the best of my knowledge, in later writings, Heidegger did not relate to, or correct, these limitations.

One major reason for the shallowness of Heidegger's rejections of the I–Thou can now be formulated. In his fundamental ontology, and in all his discussions of Dasein's Being-in-the-world, Heidegger persistently ignores the ontology of genuine meetings between persons. Hence, the worthy, enhancing, and profound human relations, such as friendship and love, that can emerge from such meetings seem to have no place in Heidegger's fundamental ontology.

As I reach the end of this brief survey of Heidegger's fundamental ontology and of his rejection of the I–Thou, two additional conclusions emerge. Both conclusions reveal major weaknesses in Heidegger's presentation of Dasein as Being-in-the-world. First, there is no evident philosophical reason for Heidegger to persistently ignore the ontology of love and of friendship. Nor is it possible to justify his ignoring of the intimacy, the mystery, and the moments of grace that can emerge in genuine meetings between persons. In his lengthy discussions of Dasein, he presents no ontological ground or any valid ontological argument that requires that we disregard genuine meetings or their ontological foundations. Indeed, there is no ontological reason for Heidegger's refusal to see, and to mention, these enhancing, worthy, and significant moments that can emerge in human relations.

Second, as pointed out in the Introduction, Heidegger was steeped in Greek philosophy. He often wrote about thoughts and ideas that the Greek thinkers, from the pre-Socratics to the post-Aristotelians, articulated. He firmly believed, and convinced me personally, that many of these thoughts can enlighten our own thinking and human existence. Thus, he was well acquainted with Plato's dialogues *Phaedrus* and *The Symposium*, which discuss the wonderful gifts of love at length. He had probably countless times read how, in these dialogues, Plato showed that love is unique to the Being of human beings. He very well understood that Plato highly praised love and linked love to wisdom. It seems, however, that nothing of Plato's enlightening and wise thoughts on love influenced Heidegger's fundamental ontology of Dasein.

I can therefore formuate a categorical statement that summarizes these seven chapters that have briefly presented Heidegger's fundamental ontology and its relation to Buber's I–Thou. In Heidegger's presentation of Dasein's fundamental ontology, Dasein's Being-with other Daseins is described and discussed without genuine meetings, and without the possibility of love and friendship. Such a description is, at best, highly problematic. My personal view is that it is severely lacking in describing the truth of human existence and hence greatly impoverishes Heidegger's fundamental ontology of Dasein.

Need I add, that by discarding love and friendship, Heidegger's fundamental ontology eliminates much that makes human existence inspiring, profound, and worthy?

NOTES

1. Martin Heidegger, *The Metaphysical Foundations of Logic*, trans. Michael Heim (Bloomington: Indiana University Press, 1984).
2. Ibid., p. 187.
3. Ibid., p. 188.

4. Ibid., p. 190.

5. For more on how poetry can illuminate such moments of grace, see Haim Gordon, *Dwelling Poetically: Educational Challenges in Heidegger's Thinking on Poetry* (Amsterdam: Rodopi, 2000).

6. Bertrand Russell, *Portraits from Memory and Other Essays* (London: George Allen & Unwin, 1956), p. 84.

PART II

BUBER'S I–THOU

Section A: I and Thou

Chapter 8

First Presentation of the I–Thou

Martin Buber first presented and described the I–Thou relationship in his short book *I and Thou*, which was published in 1923.[1] In this edition, Buber notes that the ideas presented in this book engaged him for six years; his first conception of the book occurred in 1916 and his final draft was written in 1922. *I and Thou* was soon accepted as a major contribution to both philosophy and theology. Some scholars have suggested that in this book, Buber initiated "a second Copernican revolution" in philosophical thinking, specifically in regard to the relationship between a person, as a subject, and the objects of the world.[2]

The first Copernican revolution in philosophical thinking is attributed to Immanuel Kant, who explained that the foundation of the objective world to which we relate, and of the objects in that world, can be found in human cognition. Thus, like the sun around which revolve the planets, the human subject is the central pole of the objects that exist in the objective world. The existing objects which the human subject encounters, and with them the objective world to which the subject relates, revolve around that pole. The I–Thou relationship, as described by Buber, does not and cannot fit into this Kantian model.

Buber's I–Thou is a simple human relationship in which what happens *between* the participants in the relationship is crucial. Any person can speak the primary word *Thou*. Thus, by moving the significance of what occurs to the *between, I and Thou* firmly rejects Kant's model of subject and object, in which the subject is the pole around which the objects revolve. This rejection is based on what occurs in the immediate concrete level of human existence. Whoever has spoken the basic word *Thou* during an I–Thou encounter knows that, during that moment, his or her subject was not a central pole. Put bluntly, I agree with the view, suggested by some scholars, that the prevalence of the I–Thou in interhuman relations belies Kant's Copernican revolution. For that reason, some scholars held that the I–Thou introduces a second Copernican revolution in philosophical thinking.

As is evident from my detailed presentation in previous chapters of Heidegger's fundamental ontology, which is focused on Dasein as Being-in-the-world, and on its relation to Time, his fundamental ontology also does not fit the Kantian model. Dasein is intentionally engaged in the world and establishes the world through this engaged intentionality, and through transcending its perceptions toward objects. Here there is some similarity between the thinking of Buber and that of Heidegger.

In contrast to Heidegger, however, Buber did not endeavor to present and to formulate a fundamental ontology. Nor did he raise the question of the meaning of Being as a philosophical problem that should be addressed. In some of his essays written after *I and Thou*, Buber did make some attempts to present and to describe the ontological significance of the I–Thou encounter and of dialogue. But these few attempts do not faintly resemble the establishing of a fundamental ontology, such as Heidegger endeavored to develop in *Being and Time*.

Even while thinking about the ontological status of the I–Thou, Buber's major concern was to point to a person's ability to speak the basic word *Thou* and to enter an I–Thou encounter. He described this wonderful ability and this worthy encounter using many approaches, which included prose and poetic descriptions, storytelling, and philosophical arguments. In all these approaches, he repeatedly indicated the spiritual significance of the I–Thou encounter for human existence, both on the personal level and on the levels of community and society.

Many of Buber's descriptions and articulations that focus on the I–Thou also show his readers that the I–Thou encounter unveils a possibility of human existence which had been very frequently overlooked. He calls this possibility genuine dialogue between persons. As already indicated, the citation from Bertrand Russell's memories about his meeting with Joseph Conrad, brought in Chapter 7, describes an instance of genuine dialogue. That meeting occurred some years before Buber formulated the term. This emphasis on dialogue, as linked to the I–Thou encounter, may be one reason that Martin Buber has been called the philosopher of dialogue.

* * *

Buber's presentation of the ontological status of the I–Thou emerges on the first page of *I and Thou*. Consider his opening words:

To man the world is twofold, in accordance with his twofold attitude.

The attitude of man is twofold, in accordance with the twofold nature of the primary words which he speaks.

The primary words are not isolated words, but combined words.

The one primary word is the combination *I–Thou*.

The other primary word is the combination *I–It*; wherein, without a change in the primary word, one of the words *He* and *She* can replace *It*.

Hence, the *I* of man is also twofold.

For the *I* of the primary word *I–Thou* is a different *I* from that of the primary word *I–It*.[3]

This citation, together with other formulations that appear in the first few pages of *I and Thou*, are central to Buber's presentation of the ontological status of the I–Thou. He establishes this status, however, not on the basis of a well-articulated ontological theory, but rather by pointing to human relations that persons live. Such an approach is hardly new in philosophy.

As the citation reveals, Buber opens with a description and a clarification of the distinction between the primary word *I–Thou* and the primary word *I–It*. Buber continues and explains that these primary words indicate two mutually exclusive manners of relating to beings that a person may encounter. The basic distinction is that a person speaks the primary word *I–Thou* with his or her whole being, while the primary word *I–It* is never spoken with a person's whole being. He stresses that a person's I always exists in one of these two mutually exclusive relations—either in the I–It or in the I–Thou. The I exists in, and only in, the relations that it lives.

The I–It, Buber concedes, is the relation that dominates most of human existence. Buber writes

I perceive something. I am sensible to something. I imagine something. I will something. I feel something. I think something. The life of human beings does not consist of all this and the like alone.

This and the like together establish the realm of *It*.

But the realm of *Thou* has a different basis.[4]

The realm of the It is based on what a person experiences, but experiencing, Buber indicates, means relating only with part of one's being. The realm of the Thou may come into being when a person relates to a being that the person encounters with his or her entire being. The realm of the Thou emerges when I am in full presence to the being to whom I relate, to whom I speak the primary word *I–Thou*. Let me say it again. The realm of the Thou is the realm in which I relate with my whole being.

A person can speak the primary word *I–Thou*, Buber explains, in three areas of human engagement: relations with things of nature, relations with other persons, and relations with spiritual beings such as a symphony by Mozart or a painting by Vermeer. He describes in some detail the possibility of relating to a tree as a Thou, as an example of speaking the primary word *I–Thou* to a being of nature. He emphasizes that when a person speaks the primary word *I–Thou* to any being, that person also addresses God, whom Buber calls the Eternal Thou.

An important statement in presenting the I–Thou is "The *Thou* meets me through grace—it cannot be found by seeking."[5] The meeting of the Thou in a moment of grace requires that I relate with my whole being. However, relating directly and with my whole being is not sufficient for an I–Thou moment of grace to come into being. I can endeavor, and perhaps even succeed, to relate directly and with my whole being to, say, a friend and still not speak the primary word *I–Thou*. It is a mystery and a surprise when, at a specific unprepared moment, a meeting through grace with the Thou occurs. Moments of grace are rare in any person's life. In the lives of those persons who are totally engrossed in the realm of the I–It, for instance businesspeople or politicians, moments of meeting the Thou through grace are probably very rare. In the lives of some of these persons, moments of grace may never occur.

Endeavoring to relate with my whole being is my existential choice, but I meet the Thou only when I am also chosen by a specific Thou. Buber suggests that the real life of a person is founded on such I–Thou meetings. He does not explain in detail what he means by this statement. He seems to believe that meetings with the Thou are crucial for making worthy choices in any person's life. Real life also means, for Buber, living fully in the present. I live the present fully in those wonderful, albeit rare, moments of grace when I meet the Thou. The I of the primary word *I–It* has only the past. For the I of the I–It, the present is a mere fleeting instant that it can never live fully.

Buber rejects any attempt to distance the I–Thou from concrete existence. Such distancing includes making it into an idea. Since living fully in the present occurs only in meetings with the Thou, he holds, any attempt to relegate the I–Thou, and the possibility of living in the present wholly, to the mere realm of ideas is contemptible—it erases an inspiring and blessed dimension of human existence. Put bluntly, you must endeavor to live in the present and wholly. Perhaps you may then be addressed by the Thou and encounter the Thou. In contrast, to engage in mere specualtion about the I–Thou is wrong; it may often be a mode of intellectual masturbation.

Love, according to Buber, is a real relation that can come into being only between persons who speak the primary word *I–Thou*. Feelings accompany love, they do not constitute it. Love cannot be reduced to mere feelings, since it is a relation of the whole being. A person dwells in love, Buber explains, while feelings dwell in a person.

In Part I of this book, my criticism of Heidegger's fundamental ontology often focused on his not providing an appropriate place for love in Dasein's Being-in-the-world. Heidegger's sad failure to relate to the Being of love will become distinct by looking more closely at Buber's thoughts. Thus it is appropriate to digress briefly, and to present in greater clarity and in some detail, what Buber means by love coming into being between persons who speak the primary word *I–Thou*. This digression should add support to his statements that a person dwells in love, and that feelings do not constitute love.

* * *

Testimonies to the truth of Buber's statements about love can be found in great literature and in marvelous love poems. In my discussions of love in previous chapters, I have strongly relied upon Shakespeare's *Romeo and Juliet*. A somewhat different testimony is Edgar Allan Poe's haunting love poem, "Annabel Lee," written three decades before Buber was born. Here is the full text:

Annabel Lee

It was many and many a year ago,
  In a kingdom by the sea,
That a maiden there lived whom you may know
  By the name of ANNABEL LEE;
And this maiden she lived with no other thought
  Than to love and be loved by me.

I was a child and she was a child,
  In this kingdom by the sea;
But we loved with a love that was more than love—
  I and my ANNABEL LEE;
With a love that the winged seraphs of heaven
  Coveted her and me.

And this was the reason that long ago,
  In this kingdom by the sea,
A wind blew out of a cloud, chilling
  My beautiful Annabel Lee;
So that her highborn kinsmen came
  And bore her away from me,
To shut her up in a sepulchre
  In this kingdom by the sea.

The angels not half so happy in heaven,
   Went envying her and me—
Yes!—that was the reason (as all men know,
   In this kingdom by the sea)
That the wind came out of the cloud by night,
   Chilling and killing my ANNABEL LEE.

But our love it was stronger by far than the love
   Of those who were older than we—
   Of many far wiser than we—
And neither the angels in heaven above,
   Nor the demons down under the sea,
Can ever dissever my soul from the soul
   Of the beautiful ANNABEL LEE.

For the moon never beams, without bringing me dreams
   Of the beautiful ANNABEL LEE;
And the stars never rise, but I feel the bright eyes
   Of the beautiful ANNABEL LEE;
And so, all the night-tide, I lie down by the side
Of my darling—my darling—my life and my bride,
   In her sepulchre there by the sea—
   In her tomb by the side of the sea.[6]

The first point to note is that the narrator dwells fully in his deep love for Annabel Lee. Furthermore, neither the word *feeling* nor a description of specific feelings appear in this love poem, except as a passive response, which is linked to a memory. Thus, when the stars rise, the narrator feels the bright eyes of the beautiful Annabel Lee. From the second stanza we learn that a childhood innocence characterizes the "love that is more than love" between the narrator and Annabel Lee. This childhood innocence throbs through the entire poem. As we read the poem, we can recognize that this innocence is necessary for genuine love to come into being. Buber would add that it is also necessary for speaking the primary word *I–Thou*.[7]

I wish to emphasize that Poe's "Annabel Lee" is merely one out of probably many thousands of beautiful poems and songs that testify to the truth of Buber's statements about love. Furthermore, love songs and poems are hardly a modern or contemporary phenomenon. The "Song of Songs," in the Bible, includes many exquisite love songs that describe how lovers dwell in their love. The reader will easily discern that love in the "Song of Songs" is not reduced to mere feelings. Probably more than a hundred and fifty additional examples of love poems can be found in the poetry of Pablo Neruda—he wrote a volume of one hundred love sonnets for his beloved wife, Matilda Urrutia, in addition to many other love poems. Almost all Neruda's poetry that describes love clearly shows that Buber's description of the lovers, as dwelling in their genuine love, is correct.[8]

And to return, again, to what has been discussed in previous chapters, need I add that Shakespeare's play *Romeo and Juliet*, which also includes some poetry, describes Romeo and Juliet dwelling in their love? Is it not obvious that both Romeo and Juliet relate to each other as a Thou?

Indeed, great poetry and literature repeatedly show that persons who truly love dwell in their genuine love. And this genuine love is founded on the fact that lovers speak the primary word *I–Thou* to each other, which means that the lovers can be fully present to each other. Such speaking and such presence will usually lead lovers to endeavor always to relate to each other with their entire being and as partners in dialogue. Put differently, true lovers relate to each other in the space that Buber called the between, a space that has been established between them by their speaking the primary word *I–Thou*. The situation is circular; because, in this between, they daily endeavor to speak to each other the primary word *I–Thou*.

This digression has revealed much concerning the ontological status of the I–Thou. There are many thousands of poems, stories, and songs, in many languages, written during the past three millennia which describe lovers who speak the primary word *Thou* to each other and lovers who dwell in their love. These poems, stories, and songs constitute testimonies that confirm Buber's insights. Indeed, poems, stories, and songs that describe the childhood innocence and the euphoria of true love repeatedly reveal that true lovers may undergo moments of grace together when they speak to each other with joy, as partners in dialogue. All these historical testimonies support Buber's statements concerning the I–Thou and its relationship to love.

When true lovers are lucid, they may grasp that their ability, at times, to speak the primary word *I–Thou* to each other is what establishes the dwelling place for their love. These wonderful moments of grace, to which every true lover can testify, can greatly influence a person's existence. Using two of Heidegger's terms, I can categorically state that genuine love, and speaking the primary word *I–Thou* to a loving partner in dialogue, can be central and crucial for Dasein's Being-in-the-world.

As mentioned repeatedly in previous chapters, Heidegger never seems to have discussed love in any depth. Somone might attempt to justify this lack and assume that, in his ontology, love was to be somehow fitted into Dasein's Being-with other Daseins. But, as has been repeatedly shown in previous chapters, this assumption is, at best, problematic. As the narrator in "Annabel Lee" discloses, love cannot be reduced to simply Being-with another person. Similar descriptions of the unique loving relationship appear in many poems of love. Thus love, and with it the I–Thou relationship, creates problems for Heidegger's fundamental ontology and his description of Being-with. No wonder that he discarded the I–Thou and questioned its ontological status. Unfortunately, as has been shown in preceding chapters, his attacks on the I–Thou are based on superficial and erroneous arguments.

We can abandon this brief digression and return to an abbreviated survey of *I and Thou*. Our return, however, is accompanied by a significant thought. The existence of genuine love between lovers, which often has been described in poetry, song, drama, and literature, confirms the ontological status of Buber's I–Thou.

* * *

Buber explains, in his initial description of the I–Thou, that persons cannot live always in the between established by the I–Thou. He writes that the exalted melancholy of human fate is that every Thou will eventually become an It. But, Buber intimates, the moments of I–Thou that a person has lived can continue to inspire, enhance, and influence that person's life. For instance, the memory of the specific moments of your being fully present to the Other, and of grace, can inspire your choices in new situations in which you may find yourself. Thus, the subtle or profound changes that a person may undergo during an I–Thou meeting can become beacons that guide the daily decisions of this specific person. Put differently, I–Thou meetings with spiritual beings, with other persons, or with nature may greatly enrich and deepen a person's life. They also may influence or direct the persons who have met the Thou to strive to live a worthy—Buber would say a spiritual—existence.

After the initial description of the I–Thou, and the explanation of how the I–Thou differs from the I–It, Buber's writing becomes, at times, quite problematic. He tries to show, by presenting a series of questionable assertions, that the primary word I–Thou is much more natural and prevalent in primitive communities than in contemporary society. I find his presentation very dubious and his attempts at proving his assertions totally unconvincing. Hence, I will not discuss his thoughts on this topic. Moreover, even if Buber's assertions concerning the everyday presence of the I–Thou in primitive societies were true, it means nothing about my choices and my existence here and now. A major contribution of *I and Thou* to contemporary life is to indicate that, in order to live a worthy life, I must open myself, as a person living here and now, to the possibility of speaking the primary word *Thou*. The history of the prevalence of the primary word *I–Thou* contributes nothing to the challenge facing me of speaking—or even, at times, stuttering—that primary word in my life.

Another problem emerges when Buber endeavors to explain that the newborn child, like the adult in primitive society, speaks the primary word *I–Thou* naturally. He writes of an "inborn Thou" in the newborn child; but he does not provide any valid proof or any enlightening description of the existence of this inborn tendency, or so-called instinct, to relate to the Thou. His presentation, therefore, is again dubious. Furthermore, I again would argue that whether the Thou is inborn is quite irrelevant to the simple challenge that faces me: I should direct my life in a manner that will open myself to the possibility of meeting the Thou.

Hence, I also skip this section.

* * *

In closing my presentation of the first part of *I and Thou*, I would again emphasize the mystery of the moment of grace, when an I is fully present to a Thou. This mysterious moment of grace, this presence of my whole being to the Thou, is what comes into being in an *I–Thou* meeting. This wonderful and inspiring moment of mystery, of being fully present to the Thou, can have lasting influence on the participants after the moment has faded. In some instances, such an inspiring moment can guide a person's decisions—he or she can decide to endeavor to live dialogically or to act with greater personal responsiblity in encounters in the world.

Such moments of grace, however, are not at all illuminated by Buber's rather bizarre attempts to find and to describe the I–Thou in the history of primitive societies. Nor do Buber's dubious explanations of what tendencies, or so-called instincts, exist in the soul of a newborn infant teach us anything significant about meeting the Thou here and now. Therefore, the reader of *I and Thou* must strive to learn from Buber's enlightening statements about human relations, while often brushing aside his excesses.

In closing this chapter, here is an additional enlightening statement in which Buber articulates the importance, for every person, of relating to a Thou: I become through my relation to the *Thou*.[9] This statement seems most significant for the theme of this book because it challenges Heidegger's presentation of Dasein and its quest for authenticity. Indeed, as has already been intimated in previous chapters, Buber's enlightening statement also challenges some important ideas presented in Heidegger's fundamental ontology.

NOTES

1. Martin Buber, *I and Thou*, trans. Ronald Gregor Smith (New York: Scribner's, 1958).

2. Robert E. Wood, *Martin Buber's Ontology: An Analysis of "I and Thou"* (Evanston, Ill.: Northwestern University Press, 1969), pp. xi–xii.

3. Buber, *I and Thou*, p. 3.

4. Ibid., p. 4.

5. Ibid., p. 11.

6. Edgar Allan Poe, *The Complete Poems* (New York: Dell, 1959), pp. 111–112.

7. In another work, I have shown that Heidegger's writings can teach us how to relate to poetry, including love poems and the poem "Annabel Lee." See Haim Gordon, *Dwelling Poetically: Educational Challenges in Heidegger's Thinking on Poetry* (Amsterdam: Rodopi, 2000).

8. Pablo Neruda, *100 Love Sonnets*, trans. Stephen Tapscott (Austin: University of Texas Press, 1986). Other magnificent love poems can be found in Pablo Neruda, *The Captain's Verses*, trans. Donald D. Walsh (New York: New Directions, 1972).

9. Buber, *I and Thou*, p. 11.

Chapter 9

Living the I–Thou

The second section of *I and Thou* does not add many significant ontological insights to the initial presentation of the ontology of the I–Thou and the I–It relations in the first section. Buber opens this section with a survey of human history—or with what *he* believes to be a survey of human history. In this supposed historical survey, he endeavors to broaden his previous brief description of the relationship between the I–Thou and the I–It, as it developed over the ages and as it develops in the life of a person. The major tone of pathos, together with many of the philosophical problems that are found in the second section, emerge in its opening sweeping statement:

The history of the individual and that of the human race, in whatever they may continually part company, agree at least in this one respect, that they indicate a progressive augmentation of the world of *It*.[1]

Buber provides no evidence, neither historical-factual nor ontological, to support this sweeping statement. The question arises: Why should I believe this statement?—To be blunt, I don't! What is more, my scant reading of history and my modest understanding of individual histories of persons with whom I am acquainted, and of my own history, show that Buber's statement is dubious, at best. In my own life, I might add, Buber's statement is false.

I should add that my limited experience, and my limited readings of history, have taught me that both the history of the individual and the

history of the human race are exceedingly complex. Buber should have
known that it would be very difficult, if not impossible, to substantiate
that both histories accord with his much too simple generalization. I am
unable to explain why Buber presents such a sweeping generalization.
It does not add any substance to his important appeal that, in our daily
lives, we should always be open to the possibility of relating to the Thou.
Moreover, why does Buber present additional unwarranted generalizations in the course of his discussion of the I–Thou and the I–It, and why
does he see no need to prove these general statements?

Let me briefly examine another of Buber's sweeping statements in this
section, which is again presented without supporting evidence: "Spirit
in its human manifestation is a response of man to his Thou."[2] This broad
statement immediately invites questions such as the following: And what
about the struggle for justice? Is such a struggle always a response "of
man to his Thou"? And how can you prove your statement in relation
to struggles for justice? Or would you exclude the struggle for justice
from the human manifestations of spirit? Buber's oracle-like presentation
skips bringing up all such questions.

For the record, I wish to state that there are countless examples in
history of struggles for justice that cannot be defined merely as the response of a man (or a woman) to his (or her) Thou. Here are two famous
examples from twentieth-century history.

In 1930 Mahatma Gandhi organized and personally led a three-week
march of fellow Indians from his ashram to the sea. Gandhi decided to
gather salt from the sea and thus publicly defy the unjust salt tax im-
posed by the British colonialist regime in India on the people of India.
This historical march, in which thousands of fellow demonstrators accompanied the Mahatma, was never described by Gandhi, or by any of
his colleagues who participated in the march, as a response to his Thou.
Yet that march was a step in Gandhi's ongoing nonviolent struggle for
freedom and for justice for the people of India; it was also a glorious
manifestation of human spirituality.

Much the same can be said of Nelson Mandela's many years of struggle for justice against the terrible evils of racism instigated by the wicked
apartheid regime in South Africa. His struggles for freedom and for justice for his fellow Africans—which included being jailed for 28 years—
were not a response to his Thou. It is evident that Mandela never described these difficult struggles in language which would support Buber's statement. Nevertheless, Mandela's political struggles for freedom
and justice—struggles that, he testified, constituted his life—were a spiritual engagement.

At this point, I can only whisper a word of caution to the reader.
Because unproven generalizations exist in Buber's text, the reader of the
second section of I and Thou must exercise great care. He or she must

recognize that, in this section, Buber presents quite a few unproven generalizations and sweeping statements. Hence, the sensitive reader is required to carefully separate the dross from Buber's enlightening ontological insights. In what follows, three worthy ontological insights that appear in this section and are relevant to my study of Buber's ontology are briefly presented and discussed.

* * *

Buber correctly points to two major existential dangers that hinder a life of dialogue and severely limit the possibility that a person may speak the primary word *Thou*. Both dangers are prominent in contemporary life. A person encounters the first danger when he or she is required to adhere with his or her entire being to an institution. A person may face the second danger when he or she is tempted to give primacy to his or her feelings in all interactions.

Institutions are governed by interests and almost always are concerned only with pursuing their interests. Hence, Buber states, they have no soul. Using Buber's terminology, the reason institutions have no soul is not difficult to explain. Any institution will stifle all relations which are not based on furthering its specific interests. In addition, the hierarchical interest-oriented structure of the institution, and its everyday activities in furthering those interests, provide no place or time for speaking the primary word *Thou*. Thus, the everyday laboring life of the persons who are engaged in working at, sustaining, promoting, or benefiting from the institution is always It-oriented. But both a person's soul and the soul of a community, according to Buber, emerge precisely in those dialogical relations which are *not* interest-oriented and not It-oriented. Thus, the It-oriented life of an institution has no soul.

If you are fully engrossed in your feelings, you will also find it quite impossible to relate dialogically to Others. Being engrossed in your feelings frequently means placing yourself in the center of the universe. Put differently, giving primacy to your feelings, together with your constant concern about, and your playing with, your feelings, gravely obstruct the possibility of your relating as an entire being to the Other whom you may meet. Consequently, relentless concern with and giving primacy to your feelings blocks your speaking the primary word *Thou*.

A vivid literary example of a person who is totally engrossed in his feelings is the seducer, Johannes, in Søren Kierkegaard's fictional narrative "Diary of the Seducer." This narrative is the last section of the first volume of *Either/Or*.[3] Totally engrossed in his own aestheticist way of life, Johannes delights in watching over and playing with his moods and feelings; he allows his moods and feelings to seemingly seduce him, because these moods and feelings are what make life interesting for him. Johannes also enjoys playing with the feelings and the moods of Cordelia, whom he finally seduces to spend a night with him; after that night of love, he immediately abandons her. Johannes admits that sexual intercourse hardly appeals to him. What does interest him is the process of seduction, in which he delightfully plays with his moods and feelings and with the moods and feelings of Cordelia.

Kierkegaard clearly shows the spiritual sterility of Johannes's life. His rather perverse dedication to constantly living and exploring his own moods and feelings creates a situation wherein Johannes chooses never to relate to the Other as a whole being; he chooses always to play with or to seduce other people. Johannes never shares his Being authentically with the Other. Hence, he cannot even entertain the possibility that he may love a true love, in, say, the sense of the word *love* used by Plato, Shakespeare, Poe, Neruda, and many others who have described genuine love. In stark contrast to the love described by these great writers and thinkers, a description which includes the spiritual dimensions of love, Johannes brands the appeal to his aesthetic sensitivity, coupled with the art of seduction, with the word *love*. Consequently, Johannes's life is essentially hollow.

We later readers of this great work can benefit from Buber's thinking in approaching and in learning from Kierkegaard's insights. We discern that, as long as he is totally engrossed in his moods and feelings, Johannes will not, and essentially cannot, speak the primary word *Thou*. Nor will Johannes ever establish a genuine dialogical relationship with any person. Consequently, his love is a fake.

The two above-described existential dangers which gravely hinder dialogue and the speaking of the primary word *Thou* lead Buber to issue a cautionary word of wisdom. He explains that the primary word *I–It* does not belong to the realm of evil. If, however, a person allows the primary word *I–It* to become master of his or her being, the result will be that the reality of the I, of that It-oriented person, will have been been robbed.

The reality of the I, Buber indicates many times, includes assuming responsibility for all Others to whom a person can speak the primary word *Thou*—be they beings of nature, other persons, or spiritual beings. Consequently, when the reality of the I has been robbed, a person will not speak the primary word *Thou* and will not assume responsibility for the Others whom he or she may encounter. He or she will also not assume responsibility for what occurs in the world. Usually, such a person will flee from making moral decisions. Put differently, if you decide to live fully in the I–It, you are required to eradicate the reality of your I— or to let others, say, an institution, rob the reality of your I. Following such an eradication, or robbery, of the reality of your I, you will usually not have any qualms you might have had about doing or sanctioning evil.

After the disturbing writings of Franz Kafka, which starkly illuminate the devastating effects of contemporary bureaucracy, it is hardly novel to argue that institutions very often rob the reality of the I from the persons working in them and dedicated to them. Let me present, however, a rather new and vivid bureaucratic example of robbing the reality of the I of a person; this example has recently emerged in many contemporary institutions.

Consider the name given to the department set up to deal with the persons working at many an institution. Today, in many institutions, such a department is called the Department of Human Resources. Currently, departments of human resources exist in almost every public and large capitalist institution. My university has a department of human resources. Through its name, this department enlightens us to the fact that, for that specific institution, every person working at that institution is simply a human resource. In short, by virtue of the name and the definition given to the department dealing with persons, the institution has determined that every person working in it is an It. Formally, at least, no person in an institution which boasts a department of human resources is considered to be a Thou. As Buber indicated, the reality of the I of each person has vanished; it has been robbed by the institution, for whom each specific I has become a mere resource—which is dealt with by its department of human resources. Indeed, the department of human resources, whose name fits very well with the way corporate-capitalist institutions relate to people, simply expresses the fact that contemporary capitalist and bureaucratic institutions rob the reality of the I of each person.

It is also evident that Kierkegaard's seducer, Johannes, who delights in describing and discussing in vivid detail his aesthetic Being, and his moods and feelings, robs the reality of the I of Cordelia, whom he cynically seduces and immediately abandons. The "Diary of the Seducer" reveals almost nothing about the I of Cordelia. Johannes relates to Cordelia as an It, as a being or an object that exists merely for his own pleasures, be they bodily satisfactions, intellectual illuminations about his feelings and moods, or aesthetic delights. Kierkegaard sensitively shows that Johannes does not seem to notice that, in the process of dedicating his life to enjoying and dwelling upon his own shallow feelings and insidious moods, he is letting these feelings and moods become master of his own life.

Using Buber's terminology, we can say that Johannes's unswerving dedication to his feelings and his moods has blocked the possibility of his saying the primary word *Thou*. In this process of supposed aesthetic fulfillment, Johannes's own feelings and moods have also robbed him of the reality of his own I. His dedication to his personal aesthetic fulfillment also robbed Cordelia of her I. The result is evident and accords with Kierkegaard's intention: Johannes is no profound philosophical aesthete whose feelings and moods are designed to enlighten everyone— as he would like the readers of his detailed diary to believe. He is merely one of many sordid and immoral seducers of young women. In a word, Johannes is an evil person.

* * *

Buber distinguishes between a person and an individual. An individual recognizes his or her self by being differentiated from other individuals. This differentiation is external to all individuals and it requires no particular relationship among the individuals. Thus, I can be distinguished from other individuals by the color of my hair or of my eyes, by my height and weight, and by other external features, say, my photograph or my fingerprints. Each individual is merely an object that exists among other individuals, all of whom are considered to be objects. Put succinctly, you can differentiate one individual from other individuals as you would differentiate one seashell from the bag full of seashells that you have gathered during an afternoon walk along the beach.

In contrast, you becomes aware of your being a person in speaking the primary word *Thou* or in relating dialogically to the Other. The word *person* relates to the whole being of a woman or a man and not to what differentiates this woman or that man from others. Buber's main idea here is that through genuine relations with other persons and with other beings, my own person appears and becomes real. Consequently, only by speaking the primary word *Thou* or by authentically sharing my being with those Others whom I meet in the world does the reality of my I appear. Only through such authentic sharing do I become a person. This ontological insight accords with Buber's statement, mentioned at the end of Chapter 8, that only by meeting the *Thou* does a person become an I.

Of course, I cannot always relate to each individual whom I may encounter as a person. No person can act and respond always as a whole being. But the I of the human being who persistently strives to be a genuine person, even if that I may become for a while an individual, does not lose its reality. By constantly renewing and living genuine relationships with Others, such an I again and again revives the reality of its being. Thus, the dialogical reality of the I is what may often rescue a specific I from the many travails and moments of alienation that characterize living as a mere individual.

A literary example of a dialogical and sharing person is Levin in Leo Tolstoy's novel *Anna Karenina*.[4] Surrounded by quite a few shallow and hollow individuals who are his peers and who persistently flee from relating as a whole being to Others, Levin must often relate to these alienated Others as an individual. However, he never gives up seeking moments of dialogue with Others, be they his peers or even the simple people whom he meets, such as the peasants in the countryside or the people whom he employs on his estate. By his ongoing attempts to relate dialogically to other persons and to nature, and by his being open to speaking the primary word *Thou*, Levin often revives the reality of his being. This revival ensures that he is always a person. Indeed, *Anna Karenina* engagingly shows that the reality of Levin's I is never lost or robbed. Moreover, in the course of the novel, Levin slowly matures as a person and obtains wisdom.

My previous discussion, including the example of Kierkegaard's Johannes, indicates that those human beings who are wholeheartedly dedicated to an institution or who are totally engrossed in enjoying, playing with, and reflecting upon their own feelings cannot be persons. These human beings live as individuals. I will skip a detailed description of this finding, which emerges from my above presentation.

I do want to stress again, however, that the institution does not relate to the whole being, or encourage the emergence of the whole being, of those individuals who are employed by it and dedicated to it. Nor does the man or woman who is engrossed in and relentlessly concentrates on his or her feelings live as a person. The reason for this last statement is simple and has been exemplified by Kierkegaard's seducer, Johannes. It is worth repeating, especially today when so many psychiatrists, therapists, psychologists, and even some philosophers concentrate on their clients' or adherents' feelings. These therapists, psychologists, and philosophers often forget that, if, like Johannes, you are totally engrossed in your feelings, you will not relate with your entire being to the Others whom you may meet.

* * *

The first sentences of the third section of *I and Thou* point to its central theme.

The extended lines of relations meet in the eternal *Thou*.
Every particular *Thou* is a glimpse through to the eternal *Thou*; by means of every particular *Thou*, the primary word addresses the eternal *Thou*.[5]

These first sentences are a preview of the entire section in which Buber discusses and describes a person's relationship to God, whom he calls the eternal Thou. Throughout this section, by extending and enlarging upon his ontological findings concerning the I–Thou, Buber also makes his first attempt to describe in some detail a relationship to God that is linked to worthy human relations, which stem from a person's ability to speak the primary word *Thou*.

Many laypeople and scholars have looked favorably upon this extension of interpersonal ontology to include a person's relation to God as the eternal Thou. Some have even viewed such an approach as an important breakthrough which links interpersonal relations to certain aspects of theology. Others, however, have been unhappy with Buber's vague presentation of the eternal Thou; some thinkers have also questioned the validity of his idea that the extended lines of I–Thou relations meet in the eternal Thou. This scholarly disagreement has little relevance for the theme of my study, because all the discussants agree that the I–Thou has an ontological status.

Let me enlarge briefly upon this last point. My limited experience has taught me that there is an important element of truth in Buber's statement. I have found that the moment of grace in the I–Thou encounter may point toward what may be termed the Godly. However, for the theme of this book, this truth is not very significant. Put differently, what concerns me in this study is the validity of Buber's ontological ideas and of his presentation of the I–Thou and their relevance for everyday life. For that topic, his manner of extending his ontology of interpersonal relations to include relating to the eternal Thou is not very important. Hence, I will not discuss the third section of *I and Thou*.

Still, before turning to some of Buber's other writings that deal with the I–Thou relationship, and with genuine dialogue, I want to indicate very briefly in what ways the ontological findings described in *I and Thou* reveal some basic problems in Heidegger's thinking. I also will suggest, in a most general manner, that there are areas where the ontology presented in *I and Thou* is sadly lacking. This lack in Buber's thinking emerges especially in relation to the fact that human beings are equipment-oriented in everyday life, and as such, each person is a Being-in the world. As shown, these ideas were described in much depth in Heidegger's early thinking. Some additional implications of these problems, and their ontological outcomes, will be presented in the final chapter of this book.

The reader of the chapters of this book that are dedicated to Heidegger's thinking will already have understood that the entire realm of interhuman relations presented in *I and Thou* is conspicuously lacking in Heidegger's fundamental ontology. Since Heidegger repeatedly states that in his writings he is presenting a fundamental ontology of Dasein, this lack is inexcusable. Such a presentation of the human entity—without the grandeur and the personal fulfillment that can be attained in interhuman relations through genuine dialogue and by speaking the primary word *Thou*—leaves out much that is most significant in every person's life.

A no less major problem for Heidegger's fundamental ontology is Buber's suggestion that the I–Thou relationship is primary. By that statement, he instructs us that the I–Thou encounter cannot be understood, or described, by reducing this moment of mystery and of grace to some combination of I–It relationships. This simple statement uncovers one of Heidegger's most unfortunate mistakes in criticizing the I–Thou. If you look at all the passages where he discussed and rejected the ontological status of the I–Thou, you will discover that Heidegger did not heed Buber's statement. The opposite is true. All Heidegger's attempts to reject and explain away the I–Thou, and all his explanations why we should dismiss it from any ontological discussion, were based on presenting the I–Thou as *not* being primary. Rather, Heidegger always discussed the I–Thou from his own vantage point, which pretty much ignores the unique ontological status of certain human relationships. In short, he discussed the I–Thou as if it stemmed from the primacy of I–It relationships. Such an approach is based upon a firm refusal, not upon a quest for knowledge. Yes, Heidegger refused to attempt to see the ontological foundation of human relationships, and of the dialogical aspects of human existence, to which Buber relentlessly pointed.

Look again at Heidegger's Dasein—as thrown into the world, as Being-in-the-world, as equipment-oriented, as inauthentic, as succumbing to the dictates of the "They," as care, as very frequently fleeing from the possibility of resolutely face its own death—this Dasein is described as devoid of all ontological relations to other persons. It seems to be a being that will never speak the primary word *Thou*. Even in Heidegger's presentation of care as Being-in-the-world, the possibility of relating to the Other as a Thou is missing.

Consequently, Heidegger's early writings give us an enlightening presentation of the human entity, Dasein, as an It. Each specific Dasein exists among other Its, and relates to other Its—and only to Its—that may meet it or that often intermingle with that Dasein. Note that the manners of Dasein's relating in the world, listed above, from which speaking the primary word *Thou* is missing, are some of the most basic characteristics of Dasein as Heidegger presents the human entity. Therefore, I would firmly conclude that Dasein, as Heidegger presents it, is a stunted human being.

To further press this point, I would ask, By his omitting the major dimension of interhuman existence, has not Heidegger presented Dasein as a less than fully developed human entity? Why, therefore, has he presented us with such a human entity, who may be able to raise the question of Being, who may be able to think about essences, but who is incapable of speaking the primary word *Thou?* Did he not perceive that this presentation of Dasein suggests that most persons have no other way than to live a stunted and bizarre personal existence? Did Heidegger not see that aside from moments of thinking and perhaps of resolutely facing its own death, Dasein, as he presented it, is engaged in a bleak, inauthentic, uninspiring, sordid existence? I return to some of the problems raised by these questions in the final chapter.

Buber's presentation in *I and Thou* is lacking in that he pretty much ignores the breadth and the depth of the equipment-oriented realm of human existence. As I shall soon show, such a lack in understanding the human entity is also true of much that appears in Buber's writings that were published after Heidegger's *Being and Time*. In those later writings, Buber seems never to have grasped that Heidegger's seeing of Dasein as Being-in-the-world adds much depth to our understanding of the Being of human existence. I should add that the five books by Heidegger that I have discussed in previous chapters describe and explain the significance of Dasein as Being-in-the-world and as equipment-oriented. In later writings, Heidegger continued to show that much can be understood about human existence if we begin from the perspective of Dasein as the equipment-oriented being, as the Being who establishes a world, and who can raise the question of the meaning of Being, and think about this question.

Buber's division of human existence into the realms of I–Thou and of I–It has been often criticized for being stark. It is interesting to note that even before the publication of *I and Thou*, in a personal letter to Martin Buber, Franz Rosenzweig submitted his criticism of the stark dichotomy between I–Thou and I–It that emerges in Buber's text. It seems very likely that Buber ignored this criticism; we do know that he published his text without mentioning Rosenzweig's thoughts.[6] Later, in "Elements of the Interhuman," an essay which is discussed in Chapter 10, Buber indicated that you should not view the I–Thou and the I–It as establishing a dichotomy.

In summarizing Buber's major contribution to ontology in *I and Thou*, I can state that he has pointed to the realm of the interhuman as being crucial for a worthy human existence. Learning from Buber, I would hold that any ontology of human existence should include a pointing to and discussion of a person's ability to speak the primary word *Thou*. It should also include a person's ability to estabish dialogical relations. Unfortunately, however, Buber's description of the ontology of human existence in *I and Thou* is frequently skewed toward the I–Thou, which leads to uncalled-for exaggerations.

NOTES

1. Martin Buber, *I and Thou*, trans. Ronald Gregor Smith (New York: Scribner's, 1958), p. 37.

2. Ibid., p. 39.

3. Søren Kierkegaard, *Either/Or*, vol. 1, trans. David F. Swenson and Lilian Marvin Swenson (Princeton, N.J.: Princeton University Press, 1959).

4. Leo Tolstoy, *Anna Karenina*, trans. David Magarshack (New York: Signet, 1961).

5. Buber, *I and Thou*, p. 75.

6. For more on Rosenzweig's criticism, see Bernhard Casper, "Franz Rosenzweig's Criticism of Buber's *I and Thou*," pp. 139–159 in Haim Gordon and Jochanan Bloch, *Martin Buber: A Centenary Volume* (New York: Ktav, 1984). Rosenzweig's letter can be found on pages 157–159.

Section B: Beyond I and Thou

Chapter 10

The I–Thou and Dialogue

The publication of *I and Thou* in 1923 was somewhat of a turning point in the philosophical and theological writings of Martin Buber. During the rest of his life, Buber's thinking and his scholarly work were frequently dedicated to presenting a strong foundation for the ideas first formulated in *I and Thou*. He also endeavored to develop these ideas and to describe them in greater detail. Buber often presented the foundation of the ideas he formulated in *I and Thou* in a roundabout manner. For instance, he repeatedly described the seventeenth-century Hasidim as establishing a religious community in which, quite often, authentic dialogue and genuine community prevailed. Buber also explained that interhuman dialogue, and the ongoing dialogue between God and His chosen people, are central to understanding the Hebrew Bible and even to understanding the personality and the mission of Jesus.

These scholarly studies, important as they may be to changing our understanding of human community, of Jewish history, and of biblical studies, do not add much to Buber's ontological presentation of the realm of the interhuman in *I and Thou*. However, Buber did write a few essays in which he attempted to add to his description of the I–Thou and of genuine dialogue and to broaden and deepen the foundations of the concept of the I–Thou encounter. He also endeavored to better explain and describe the significance of dialogue in everyday life.

In this chapter, I briefly describe what may be learned about Buber's ontological thinking from four of these essays. I have chosen the essays which seem to me the most significant of his ontological writings on the status of the I–Thou. Chapter 11 will discuss Buber's essay "What Is Man?" In that essay Buber presents additional ontological thoughts and writes extensively about Heidegger; the essay includes a firm rejection of Heidegger's fundamental ontology.

Before turning to the four essays which were written to support the ideas presented in *I and Thou*, I want to clarify the distinction between an I–Thou encounter and a genuine dialogical relationship. In a genuine dialogical relationship, I relate to my partner in dialogue as a person with whom I share this world and this specific meeting between us. I make no attempts to manipulate my partner in dialogue; nor do I attempt to manipulate the relationship or the conversation that arises between us. Nor is any empathy involved in my relating to my partner in dialogue. I listen carefully and wholeheartedly to what my partner in dialogue wishes to share with me, and, while conversing with my partner, I strive to relate with my entire being to his or her whole being. To relate to the whole being of my partner in dialogue I must confront him or her with my whole being. This act of confronting with my whole being is crucial. Without such confronting genuine dialogue will not emerge.

The I–Thou encounter can arise out of genuine dialogue, but it also may emerge, suddenly, even out of a moment of indifference. Indeed, this wonderful moment of grace can also come into being with a person who never was a partner in dialogue. Buber mentions that it can occur, for a brief silent moment, when two persons' eyes meet on a city bus before one of them leaves the bus at his or her station. Let me reiterate this point. The I–Thou encounter, the speaking of the primary word *Thou*, surprises both participants, since it is a spontaneous unplanned moment that arises through grace. In this inspiring and enhancing moment, both participants in the encounter are fully present to each other.

Of course, the I–Thou encounter can help to establish an attitude that encourages geunine dialogue. After a person has spoken the primary word *Thou* to another person in an I–Thou encounter, or after he or she has encountered the Thou of a natural being or of a spiritual being, quite often such a person will strive to relate to others as partners in dialogue. Thus, an I–Thou encounter often enhances the everyday mode of being of the participants. It may influence them to relate to many other persons whom they may meet in the course of everyday life as partners in dialogue and as persons to whom they are willing to speak the primary word *Thou*.

* * *

Buber's essay "Dialogue" was first published in 1929. He later explained that the essay "proceeded from the desire to clarify the 'dialogical' principle presented in *I and Thou*, to illustrate it and to make it precise in relation to essential spheres in life."[1] My impression from the essay is that Buber's desire to clarify the dialogical principle presented in *I and Thou* is not fulfilled. Rather, the essay strews quite a bit of confusion. It is often written in oracularlike prose, without convincing proofs, or well-thought arguments, or apt descriptions that support the ideas presented.

For instance, Buber writes "Each one of us is encased in armour whose task is to ward off signs."[2] My impression from the essay is that the signs to which Buber is referring are what may be termed emanations of the wish for dialogue that emerge from all the beings in the world. He holds that these emanations, these signs of the wish for dialogue, are always present for whoever would care to perceive them and relate to them. However, each and every person is "encased in an armour whose task is to ward off signs."

But perturbing questions immediately emerge. How does Buber know about the signs? How does Buber know about this armor? How does he know that every person is encased in this armor? How does he know that the signs exist, since each one of us, including Martin Buber himself, is supposedly encased in armor that wards off the signs? He never tells us.

As I did in Chapter 9, I must again point out that a sweeping statement, such as Buber's assertion concerning our being encased in armor, requires either factual evidence or ontological description to support it. No such supporting factual statements or ontological descriptions appear in Buber's essay "Dialogue." Nor have I found support for this statement in his other writings. Hence, I would question the validity of this sweeping statement and with it the validity of the ontological reality of the "signs" and the "armor" which seems to underlie the statement. Unfortunately, such sweeping statements appear quite frequently in the essay "Dialogue."

Sweeping statements are not Buber's only failing in this essay. In his continual quest to enlarge the scope of the I–Thou relationship, Buber contradicts an important statement that he presented in *I and Thou*. The statement concerns thinking. In *I and Thou*, thinking belonged to the realm of the It. In my citation from *I and Thou* in Chapter 8 (at note 3), Buber clearly explains that thinking belongs to the realm of the It. In contrast, in "Dialogue" Buber suggests that thinking is essentially a relationship between I and Thou.[3] To support this suggestion, he cites seemingly supporting passages from writings by Wilhelm von Humboldt and Ludwig Feuerbach. However, Buber does not mention that, in thus describing the act of thinking, he is contradicting what he wrote in *I and Thou*.

Furthermore, Buber's suggestion is wrong; among other reasons, because all major thinkers from Plato through Aquinas and Descartes to Heidegger have described thinking quite differently. In all these philosophers' writings, thinking does not require relating to the Thou. Not one of these major thinkers suggested that thinking is in any way linked to speaking the primary word *Thou*. Buber here blatantly ignored the wisdom of many great predecessors. However, Buber is also basically wrong for the simple reason that every person who has attempted to think will recognize that thinking is primarily a solitary activity. While a person is thinking there is no speaking of the primary word *Thou* to the Other. Usually, there is no speaking at all, and the Other becomes marginal. When Socrates sank into thinking, Plato writes, he stood silent for hours, not even hearing the people who spoke to him.

At this point, I can formulate my reservations with two questions. Why did Buber not mention the contradiction between what he wrote about thinking in "Dialogue" and what he wrote about it in *I and Thou?* Why did he blatantly ignore counterexamples to his suggestion on what constitutes thinking, such as Plato's description of Socrates while he was thinking? My answer to both questions is: I do not know.

Alongside these and other failings in "Dialogue," Buber does present a worthy tale which illuminates and adds some depth to his ontological thinking:

There is a tale that a man inspired by God once went out from the creaturely realms into the vast waste. There he wandered till he came to the gates of the mystery. He knocked. From within came the cry: "What do you want here?" He said, "I have proclaimed your praise in the ears of mortals, but they were deaf to me. So I come to you that you yourself may hear me and reply." "Turn back," came the cry from within. "Here is no ear for you. I have sunk my hearing in the deafness of mortals."[4]

This haunting tale can have many worthy interpretations. An interpretation which I prefer, and which accords with Buber's thinking, points to the difficulty of relating dialogically and of speaking the primary word *Thou*. Many people have chosen to be deaf to the articulations of the person who wishes to relate dialogically to them or to proclaim the mystery, say, of the I–Thou encounter. Indeed, my personal experience again and again reveals to me that many people choose to be deaf when I wish to relate dialogically to them. The story suggests, however, that frequently it is precisely to those people who have chosen to be deaf to the primary word *Thou*, and who firmly reject dialogue, that the person of dialogue must relentlessly appeal. Thus, the tale helps Buber depict some of the very discouraging difficulties that a person who wishes to live a life of dialogue may encounter.

The tale, therefore, teaches me that if I want to live a life of dialogue, I must recognize that my attempts to relate dialogically to other persons will frequently fail. However, I must never give up the strenuous struggle to arouse the hearing of those possible partners in dialogue who have chosen to be deaf to dialogue. I must always remember that their deafness to the primary word *Thou* is a way of life that these purposely deaf people chose; deafness to dialogue is a flight from the ontological possibility of relating dialogically. This conclusion is worth repeating: Deafness to the primary word *Thou* and to genuine dialogue is a personal choice.

In summary, I would hold that, aside from this tale and its valid implications, the essay "Dialogue" does not add any substantial ontological ideas or insights to *I and Thou*.

* * *

Buber's essay "The Question to the Single One" was written on the basis of a lecture that he presented in 1933.[5] The essay was published in book form in Germany in 1936. In this essay, Buber questions and criticizes Kierkegaard's concept of the whole person as the Single One who faces God and relates to Him. The essay has aroused some criticism, especially among Kierkegaard scholars, who claim that Buber did not read Kierkegaard carefully.[6]

Perhaps, as these scholars hold, Buber did not sense all the nuances about human relations that may be found in Kierkegaard's multiple writings. However, Buber is essentially correct in pointing out that Kierkegaard's writings pretty much ignored the possibility of a person speaking the primary word *Thou*. Nor did Kierkegaard clearly present the idea that establishing genuine dialogue with other persons is crucial to relating as a whole being to those persons and to establishing worthy relations with them. Buber is also correct in holding that central to Kierkegaard's writings is the solitary person, as a Single One, who is often very alone while facing God.

In this essay, Buber also correctly stresses the ontological importance of interhuman relations in learning to relate to God. Put succinctly, Buber once again explains that a person who wishes to relate as a whole being to God—such a person dare not ignore the Other whom he may meet. He or she must strive to relate to this Other dialogically, as a possible Thou. Only when a person strives to relate fully and wholeheartedly to the Other can a meaningful relationship with God come into being. Thus, in this essay Buber shows that, at least, his ontology of the I–Thou adds important dimensions to Kierkegaard's thinking. It adds the insight that there is a definite link between interhuman relations and the relation between a person and God. The essay also shows—and this was one of Buber's major intentions—that there are no few problems with Kierkegaard's concept of the Single One. I shall not discuss these problems, since they would take us too far astray.

I should add, however, that Buber's essay on Kierkegaard is relevant to my study because, quite often, Heidegger's presentation of Dasein, which I have presented in previous chapters, seems very close to Kierkegaard's ideas concerning the Single One. In a nutshell, Buber's thinking in this essay shows that both Heidegger and Kierkegaard were mistaken when they ignored the dialogical dimension of human existence and the possibility of a person speaking the primary word *Thou*.

However, "The Question to the Single One" also reveals a major problem in Buber's ontological thinking. It has to do with Buber's distorted, and often inauthentic, relationship to what occurs in the political realm. Here, I can only point very briefly to this mistake and hint at its ontological significance.[7]

Buber discusses the political realm after pointing out that he understands Good as direction and Evil as lack of direction. These explanations immediately raise disturbing questions such as, Was the Evil performed in Auschwitz merely a result of lack of direction? Was the Evil of the apartheid regime in South Africa merely a result of lack of direction? And, to return to ontology, is the Evil that a person or a regime performs merely a result of lack of direction? Why does Buber refuse to be more specific?

Evil, as I learned from Jean-Paul Sartre and from my many years of struggles for the human rights of Israelis and Palestinians, is a purposeful destruction of human freedom. Armed with Sartre's definition, I have also studied some of the manifestations of Evil in Israel and in the world and have described my findings in three other books.[8] My studies of Evil lead to the conclusion that Buber's definition of Evil is very mistaken and his discussion of Evil, here and in other writings, is indeed shallow. Perhaps this shallowness is the reason that Buber provides no specific examples of social or political Evil.

But even if we acknowledge a meager element of truth in Buber's formulations, consider what he has to say about politics. He explains that while for ethics there exist the poles of Good and Evil,

For the realm of the political there is no pair of concepts in the foreground, obviously because it is more difficult, or impossible to give autonomy to the negative pole in it. I should call the pair in the background order and absence of order. . . . Right order is direction and form in the political realm.[9]

In this quotation, Buber is very wrong. There does exist a pair of concepts in the foreground of the political realm which illuminates the worthiness of human activity in this realm. The pair is justice and injustice. I want to counter Buber's writings much more straightforwardly. I want to state categorically that the struggle for justice and the pursuit of justice within the political realm is a most worthy human endeavor. I would firmly add, again contradicting Buber, that the importance and the grandeur of the political realm is, precisely, that in this realm persons can pursue justice.

Moreover, as Buber should have known well, the pair of concepts justice and injustice has been in the foreground of politics and of political thinking for millennia. Does Buber need to be reminded that Moses demanded, in the Bible, that the Children of Israel, as a nation, as a political entity, and as individuals, daily pursue justice?

What is more, a passing look at many philosophical texts of the past two and a half millennia, even while ignoring religious revelations linked to justice such as Moses bringing down the Decalogue from Mount Sinai, discloses Buber's superficial ideas. In these philosophical texts, we will find that the link of justice and injustice to the political realm has been prominent in philosophical thinking for at least twenty-five centuries. Justice was discussed in ancient Greece, by Hesiod and others, many years before Plato wrote his *Republic*, which deals explicitly with the pursuit of justice in the political realm.

Why did Buber discuss the political realm and blatantly ignore justice and injustice? I do not know. Has his blatant ignoring of justice, and of the struggle for justice in the political realm, important ontological implications? I believe it has.

In struggling for justice, in fighting Evil in the political realm, human intentionality and a person's resolution in face of one's own death, as Heidegger presented these concepts, are often crucial. Since the pursuit of justice is not the topic of this book, developing this theme would take me much too far astray. I can say that, ontologically, realizing justice in the political realm often requires that a person relate to Others in the equipment-oriented manner that Heidegger discussed, and with the personal resolution that he articulated. I want to stress this last point. Struggling for justice very often means facing and fighting Evil resolutely, and that could mean facing one's own death resolutely.

To be specific, struggling for justice today, say, against the many evil global corporations who are today ruining the lives of millions of persons in the world, in addition to destroying the world's flora and fauna, is *not* based on, or linked to, genuine dialogue or to I–Thou relationships. The opposite is the case. The struggle for justice against these powerful and cynical evildoers, and their many supporters in the capitalist-oriented governments, occurs in the political realm, that is, in the realm of I–It. Buber's definition of Good and Evil and his presentation of what characterizes the political realm are hindrances to such a struggle.

Perhaps we have found in the above paragraph a hint of the reasons Buber ignores the centrality of justice to political activity. My impression is that Buber frequently tried, here and in other writings, to diminish the significance of all and any Good that can emerge in the realm of the I–It. But proving this point would, again, take us astray.

Another way in which Buber diminishes the significance of human activity in the realm of the I–It, in "The Question to the Single One" and in other writings, is his emphasis on the so-called dichotomy between individualism and collectivism. Individualism, according to Buber, emerges when an individual perceives oneself as central to all decisions and activities that one must undertake and acts accordingly; collectivism emerges when an individual gives up one's freedom to choose and act and allows an organization to decide for him or her. Buber rejects both individualism and collectivism as not allowing the whole being of a person to develop. Granted. In its stead, he suggests that we should emphasize living dialogical relations with other persons.

Such a suggestion is wonderful. But, as the above paragraphs suggest, it overlooks one quite important problem. In the pursuit of justice, in the struggle for justice, dialogical relations very rarely bring about major changes. You have to remember that Socrates frequently strove to relate dialogically to his fellow Athenians, even by Buber's standards. But this same Socrates was put to death, after a trial in Athens, by the Athenians to whom he strove to relate dialogically. His condemnation and his death sentence were a result of his ongoing daily struggle in Athens for wisdom and for justice. We, who are much less talented than Socrates, must learn from his sad plight that in struggling for wisdom and for justice, dialogue does not always help. Once again, Buber's suggestions and conclusions ignore the importance of the nondialogical struggle for justice in the political realm.

To recapitulate, Buber's critique and disparaging of the political realm in "The Question to the Single One" is shallow and ontologically mistaken. It is sad that Buber hardly ever acknowledged that the grandeur of human existence does not emerge only in interhuman dialogue or in I–Thou relations. Human freedom and grandeur also emerge in worthy political activity, especially in the struggle for justice. Think again of Mahatma Gandhi and Nelson Mandela.

* * *

Buber wrote the short essay "Elements of the Interhuman"[10] some thirty years after *I and Thou*. In accordance with its name, in this essay he presents some of the elements of the realm of that he calls the interhuman. The interhuman is the realm in which genuine dialogue and I–Thou relations can come into being. This realm, Buber explains, cannot be reduced to psychology, sociology, anthropology, or any other behavioral or social science; it is an independent realm of human existence. Many of the most important events in a persons's life, such as falling in love, occur in the interhuman realm.

In this essay, Buber also explicitly, and at times implicitly, suggests how a person must endeavor to live so as to establish dialogical relations with others and be open to the possibility of speaking the primary word *Thou*. Thus, the essay also has some major educational implications. In a book that I wrote more than fifteen years ago, on the basis of my personal experience as an educator, I described the relevance to education, and especially to education for dialogue and for peace, of some of the ideas that Buber presented in "Elements of the Interhuman."[11] In that book, however, I did not focus upon the significance of the ontological insights of the essay.

Viewed from an ontological perspective, "Elements of the Interhuman" helps Buber show how simple everyday decisions, attitudes, and choices of a way of life can hinder or can assist a person who wishes to live a life of dialogue. He clearly describes different areas of life in which a person's everyday decisions, attitudes, and choices are linked to the possibility of speaking the primary word *Thou* and to the possibility of relating dialogically to other persons. For instance, Buber distinguishes between being and seeming. Seeming, in Buber's terminology, means trying to make a particular, usually favorable, impression upon other persons. Being means endeavoring to present yourself as you truly are. In explaining the difference between being and seeming, Buber makes a rather clear distinction: "We may distinguish between two different types of human existence. The one proceeds from what one really is, the other from what one wishes to seem."[12]

It is not difficult to apprehend that for genuine dialogue to come into being, a person must endeavor to relate to others as "one really is" and not as "one wishes to seem." Such a decision, Buber admits, often requires courage and straightforwardness. But without such a striving to relate as "one really is," dialogue is pretty much doomed to fail. Persons who are steeped in seeming, persons who care only about the impression that they make upon others, cannot and will not relate dialogically to each other. Many, if not most, politicians are steeped in seeming. Furthermore, a person who relates as "one really is" will probably be inclined much more to speak the primary word *Thou* than a person who relates as "one wishes to seem" and merely strives to make a certain impression upon others.

I will not present all Buber's pertinent suggestions on how genuine dialogue and the I–Thou are linked to certain everyday decisions and attitudes toward life. I do wish to reiterate, however, that "Elements of the Interhuman" clearly shows how specific decisions, attitudes, and choices of a daily mode of existence are linked to the ontological insights of *I and Thou*. This short essay, therefore, reveals the relevance of Buber's ontological findings in *I and Thou* to a person's simple choices and to his or her chosen behavior in everyday life. Consequently, "Elements of the

Interhuman" adds much support, from the realm of everyday existence, to many truths in Buber's ontology of the I–Thou relationship and of genuine dialogue.

* * *

Buber's ontological essay "Distance and Relation" was published in 1951.[13] In this essay Buber presents what he believes are two basic ontological movements that are components of the principle of human existence. The first movement is "the primal setting of a distance" between the person and other beings that are present and constitute the person's world. The second movement is "entering into a relation."[14] The first movement, Buber adds, presupposes the second movement, because a person can enter into a relation only with a being that has been set at a distance.

Although this essay does give an additional ontological perspective to the emergence of dialogue, there is very little that is novel or thought-provoking or profound about its major ideas. Similar thoughts, albeit in a somewhat different terminology, had been expressed a few years previously by thinkers such as Maurice Merleau-Ponty, Jean-Paul Sartre, and especially Martin Heidegger. In particular, since Buber discusses the relationship of the human entity to the world, it is very strange that he did not acknowledge the existence of Heidegger's concept of Dasein as Being-in-the-world. It seems very dubious to me that Buber's blatant disregarding of Heidegger's concept was mere oversight.

Moreover, my discussion of Heidegger's Dasein as Being-in-the-world, in previous chapters of this study, suggests that this concept includes what Buber calls the primal setting of a distance and the entering into a relation that establishes a world. It is also evident that Dasein, as Being-in-the-world, establishes a world through entering into relations with other beings and persons. Hence, I find it particularly unfortunate that in "Distance and Relation" Buber discussed a person's primal relation to the world and ignored Heidegger's concept of Being-in-the-world.

I want to emphasize again that there is no excuse for Buber's ignoring Heidegger's thinking on the primal relation of Dasein to the world, especially since in 1938 Buber discussed and attacked ideas found in *Being and Time* at some length in his essay "What Is Man?" (As mentioned, Buber's response to Heidegger's thinking in "What Is Man?" will be discussed in the next chapter.)

I therefore can conclude that the essay "Distance and Relation" might give a new perspective on dialogue; but it does not add new substantial insights to Buber's ontological findings that were expressed in *I and Thou*. Nor does the essay challenge any of Heidegger's ontological insights concerning Dasein as Being-in-the-world.

* * *

My very brief survey of four essays that Buber wrote to support the ontology described in *I and Thou*, and to "clarify the dialogical principle presented in *I and Thou*," has not yielded very encouraging results. In "Elements of the Interhuman," Buber did present a few new important ontological ideas and insights on the links between a person's everyday existence and the possibility of living a life of dialogue; these ideas also have relevance to the possibility of speaking the primary word *Thou*. In "The Question to the Single One," Buber showed some basic problems in Kierkegaard's ontology. He revealed that Kierkegaard's thinking is quite lacking because he ignored genuine dialogue and did not relate to the possibility of speaking the primary word *Thou*. But in this same essay, Buber's own ideas on Good and Evil and on the political realm are quite wrong.

Buber's two other essays, "Dialogue" and "Distance and Relation," may at times be interesting. But they also include quite a few philosophical problems, mistakes, and shortcomings. In addition, these two essays yield very few new ontological insights that go beyond what can be learned from *I and Thou*.

NOTES

1. Martin Buber, Foreword to *Between Man and Man*, trans. Ronald Gregor Smith (Boston: Beacon Press, 1955), p. vii.

2. Martin Buber, "Dialogue," in *Between Man and Man*, p. 10.

3. Ibid., pp. 26–27.

4. Ibid., p. 15.

5. Martin Buber, "The Question to the Single One," in *Between Man and Man*.

6. See, for instance, Robert L. Perkins, "Buber and Kierkegaard: A Philosophical Encounter," in Haim Gordon and Jochanan Bloch, *Martin Buber: A Centenary Volume* (New York: Ktav, 1984), pp. 275–303.

7. For more on problems in Buber's political thinking, see Haim Gordon, "Existential Guilt and Buber's Social and Political Thought," in Gordon and Bloch, *Martin Buber*, pp. 215–232.

8. Haim Gordon, *Quicksand: Israel, the Intifada, and the Rise of Political Evil in Democracies* (East Lansing: Michigan State University Press, 1995). Haim Gordon and Rivca Gordon, *Sartre and Evil: Guidelines for a Struggle* (Westport, Conn.: Greenwood Press, 1995). Haim Gordon, *Fighting Evil: Unsung Heroes in the Novels of Graham Greene* (Westport, Conn.: Greenwood Press, 1997).

9. Buber, "The Question to the Single One," p. 75.

10. Martin Buber, "Elements of the Interhuman," in *The Knowledge of Man*, trans. Maurice Friedman and Ronald Gregor Smith (New York: Harper & Row, 1965).

11. Haim Gordon, *Dance, Dialogue, and Despair: Existentialist Philosophy and Education for Peace in Israel* (Tuscaloosa: University of Alabama Press, 1986).

12. Buber, "Elements of the Interhuman," pp. 75–76.

13. Martin Buber, "Distance and Relation," in *The Knowledge of Man*.

14. Ibid., p. 60.

Chapter 11

Buber's Critique of Heidegger

Buber gave the title "What Is Man?" to a long essay that he published, which was based on his innaugural course of lectures as professor of social philosophy at the Hebrew University in Jerusalem in 1938.[1] In the spring of 1938, Buber and his family had emigrated from Nazi Germany to Palestine and settled in Jerusalem, where Buber had been called to the Chair of Social Philosophy at the Hebrew University. A section of the essay "What Is Man?" is dedicated to an extensive critique of ideas from Heidegger's books, especially *Being and Time*.

The bulk of Buber's essay is a historical survey of approaches to answering the question "what is man?" The survey is often accompanied by philosophical critique. The essay indicates that Buber took the question from Immanuel Kant's writings. But, according to Buber, Kant merely posed the question and never suggested a worthy philosophical-anthropological response. Buber believes that the question "what is man?" is at the basis of the field that he calls philosophical anthropology, which is the field that should discuss and illuminate the being of the whole person.

In his essay, Buber endeavors to show that, in the history of Western thought, the question "what is man?" much too often has been evaded, misunderstood, or mistakenly answered. One reason for these faulty responses, he indicates, is that most thinkers did not consider and discuss what may be called the realm of the interhuman. Another reason is that there are inherent difficulties in discussing the whole person. Such can be seen from the fact that the scientific approach, and also many philosophers, usually deal with a part of the whole person. For instance, psychologists and philosophers have discussed the psychology of imagination. Another common way of not discussing the whole person is viewing him or her as a part of a larger entity, say, when someone does research on the roles of women as members of a religious community.

In the essay, Buber suggests that there are certain historical periods in which human beings find themselves to be solitary in society and in the cosmos, and therefore they raise this question "what is man?" In contrast, during periods when a person feels that he or she has a fixed and ensured place in the cosmos and in society, usually the question "what is man?" is not raised. I will not present Buber's historical survey of Western thought, nor will I discuss the philosophical or historical validity of his survey. I can say that I have not found Buber's historical-philosophical survey very enlightening or thought-provoking. I do want to examine, quite briefly, Buber's presentation and critique of Heidegger's thinking.

* * *

The second section of Buber's essay "What Is Man?" is called "Modern Attempts." In that section Buber dedicates an entire chapter to what he calls "The Doctrine of Heidegger."[2] In this chapter, Buber discusses *Being and Time*. From the beginning of this chapter, however, Buber seems to foist upon Heidegger certain views that are very foreign to Heidegger's thinking.

For instance, Buber ignores the fact that Heidegger writes about Dasein, as the entity which I am, that is, as the human entity that is engaged in the world. He suggests that the only matter that interests Heidegger is existence. Here is an example of one of Buber's key opening sentences in which he criticizes Heidegger's fundamental ontology: "fundamental ontology does not have to do with man in his actual manifold complexity, but solely with existence in itself, which manifests itself through man."[3] Even for the reader who has not read *Being and Time*, and who has merely braved the first three chapters of this book, it is not difficult to perceive that this sentence is a gross misinterpretation of what Heidegger wrote. Buber's statement also testifies to his very shallow reading of *Being and Time*.

To illuminate Buber's mistake, the reader should recall that, in the first three chapters, I have shown that in *Being and Time* Heidegger raises the question of the meaning of Being. To approach that question in the best possible and most lucid way, he understands that he has to develop a fundamental ontology of the human entity, whom he terms Dasein. The reason for developing this fundamental ontology is that among all the known beings that exist, only Dasein can raise the question of the meaning of Being. Thus, by developing a fundamental ontology of Dasein, of the only being who can raise the question of the meaning of Being, Heidegger believes that we may be able to gain better access to the question of the meaning of Being. But, as I have repeatedly shown in those chapters, Heidegger's fundamental ontology of Dasein stands on its own feet. It contributes substantially to our undersanding of the human entity, even without evaluating whether Heidegger succeeded in raising the question of the meaning of Being. As many, many scholars have agreed, *Being and Time* is most important in partially enlightening the existence and the daily life of the human entity.

At this point, Buber's gross mistake in the above citation becomes evident. The fundamental ontology of Dasein, as Heidegger presents it in detail, does have to do with the human entity in its "actual manifold complexity." In previous chapters, I have given quite a few examples that support Heidegger's fundamental ontology; let me remind the reader of merely one crucial literary example. Recall the soliloquy from Shakespeare's *Hamlet* in Chapter 3. My discussion of how this soliloquy accords with Heidegger's thinking about Dasein clearly shows the superficiality of Buber's critique in his cited statement. After all, Hamlet is presented by Shakespeare with all his "actual manifold complexity." We, as readers of the play or as spectators of the tragedy in the theater, can learn much from Hamlet's plight and struggles—because the description of his actual manifold complexity illuminates situations in which we may find ourselves or are analogous to situations which we might encounter. Furthermore, as I suggested in Chapter 3, Heidegger's fundamental ontology helps us better to comprehend Hamlet's terrible plight and his courageous decision to face his own death resolutely, authentically.

In short, Buber begins his first criticism of Heidegger's fundamental ontology with a grave mistake.

* * *

This mistake, however, should not diminish the impact of Buber's important and valid criticisms of *Being and Time*. As my discussions of Heidegger's books in previous chapters have shown, Buber is correct when he points out, in "What Is Man?" that Heidegger's fundamental ontology pretty much ignores the wonderful possibilities of human dialogue. Buber correctly stresses that, since the possibilities inherent in dialogue greatly enhance human existence, there is a sterile element in Heidegger's presentation of Dasein.

Buber is also right in repeatedly pointing out that Dasein, as presented by Heidegger, is hardly concerned with life in the realm of the inter-human, or with the possibility of an I–Thou encounter. Hence, an entire dimension of human existence seems to be missing in *Being and Time*. (As has been shown, it is also missing in the other books that I have discussed in previous chapters.) Furthermore, Buber correctly holds that Heidegger's mistaken approach reaches a rather grotesque extremity when he describes Being-guilty without relating the guilt of Dasein to its relations with other people or to the social and political realities in which Dasein finds itself.

In previous chapters, I have shown that genuine dialogue is not mentioned by Heidegger, especially where it seems to be natural to discuss dialogue—say, in his discussion of Dasein's Being-with other Daseins. Thus, Buber's harsh criticism of what he terms the monological presentation of Dasein as Being-in-the-world is very well founded. Buber is also correct when he criticizes Heidegger for stressing that Dasein can start to be authentic only if it faces its own death resolutely. That is an extremely narrow view of human existence, Buber explains.

Need I add that many of Buber's writings point to other possibilities of starting to be authentic, among them the joy of life which can be expressed in genuine dialogue and moments of true faith in God? Heidegger, of course, ignored such moments, and Buber justly criticizes him for his narrow perspective of human existence. Furthermore, as I have indicated repeatedly in the course of this book, and in other writings, genuine dialogue, love, and friendship, which can also lead to an authentic and worthy existence, are never mentioned by Heidegger.

* * *

Heidegger's grave mistake in ignoring the realm of the interhuman, however, does not justify the many mistakes made by Buber in his essay. These mistakes repeatedly appear in Buber's discussion of certain aspects of *Being and Time*. Probably Buber's worst mistake is his not seeing that, despite the shortcomings of *Being and Time*, despite its ignoring the dialogical dimension of personal existence, in this volume Heidegger has presented many profound insights concerning our daily life. To mention just one insight that Buber blatantly ignored, he never mentions the significance of Heidegger's discussion of truth as aletheia and his describing Dasein's existence as a discloser and uncoverer of truth. Keeping this failing in mind, the question to Buber immediately arises: Is not the human relationship to truth central to answering the philosophical-anthropological question "what is man?"

Buber's many mistakes concerning Heidegger's thinking in his essay are all the more disturbing because, at times, he purposely seems to have embraced myopia. From what I wrote in the first three chapters, it is immediately evident that the many profound insights found in *Being and Time* cannot and should not be brushed aside if the question addressed in Buber's essay, that is, the question concerning a person's whole being, is to be honestly addressed. Put differently, I firmly hold, and the three chapters dedicated to *Being and Time* support my view, that many of

Heidegger's insights concerning the mode of existence of Dasein do provide an important, if partial, answer to Buber's philosophical-anthropological question "what is man?" I will not attempt to prove this assertion in detail here.

Nevertheless, in order to be fair to Heidegger, I will formulate my support of Heidegger's many important insights and ideas with three additional questions that Buber should have asked himself when reading and pondering the ideas found in *Being and Time*: Is it not true that Dasein, the human entity, is the only being that can raise the question of the meaning of Being? And does not Dasein's ability to raise the question of the meaning of Being, as shown in detail in *Being and Time*, partially unveil the whole being of Dasein? Does not this partial unveiling of the whole being of Dasein provide a partial answer to the question "what is man?"

As mentioned, Buber ignored these crucial questions. But the questions emerge in even a first reading of Buber's critique of *Being and Time*.

On second thought, one additional point that reveals Buber's myopia concerning the valuable insights in *Being and Time* should be mentioned. Buber seems not to have wanted to admit that there is much to be learned from Heidegger's description of Dasein as existing in equipment-oriented human society. Since the beginning of history, however, the fact that human beings are equipment-oriented has been a basic characteristic of several historical societies, periods, and ages. Locutions, definitions, and phrases used by historians—such as the hunter society, the Bronze Age, the age of gunpowder, the period following the discovery of the printing press, the information society—all testify to the importance of equipment for the being of humans as historical beings. Put differently, for historians there is no question that human history, to a large extent, is and has been governed by the fact that Dasein is equipment-oriented.

Let me state again that Buber does not want to comprehend the existential implications of this empirical fact, of Dasein being equipment-oriented. One sad result of Buber's ignoring such a historically accepted fact is that his criticism of *Being and Time* often has a hollow ring. Why did Buber refuse to discuss the ontological and empirical fact that persons are equipment-oriented? Why did he refuse to acknowledge that this orientation can help us to answer the question "what is man?"— I have no answers, except to point again to his purposely embraced myopia.

Someone may ask, What do you mean when you state that Buber's criticism of *Being and Time* often has a hollow ring? One answer has already been given. Buber's blatant ignoring of the fact that Dasein is an equipment-oriented being is a pertinent example that already reveals hollowness. I will give one additional example—at least a dozen could be mustered.

Buber presents quite fairly what Heidegger has said about the "They" and its influence on making the daily life of most people inauthentic. But when he summarizes this section of *Being and Time*, as the following quotation reveals, his judgment falters. To understand the following quotation I should add that in the standard translation of *Being and Time* into English, Heidegger's term "das Man" is translated as "the They." Buber accepted the translation of "das Man" in the following citation as "the one."

What Heidegger says about the "one" [the "They"] and a man's relation to it is right in its essential traits. It is also right that a man has to disengage himself from it in order to reach self-being. But something is lacking here, without which what is right in itself becomes wrong.[4]

Buber does not say clearly what is lacking in Heidegger's presentation of the "They." From a close reading of the paragraphs that follow this brief quotation, I can safely assume that Buber condemns Heidegger's discussion of the "They" because in his discussion he did not relate to the I–Thou encounter and to genuine dialogue. Again we are confronted with a purposeful vagueness that characterizes Buber's writings, a vagueness I already mentioned in the Introduction to this book. Let me add that here the vagueness is irresponsible; because Buber states that Heidegger's right insights become wrong without presenting a well-argued proof or a valid description to support his statement. Such vagueness and irresponsibility are often behind Buber's hollow statements.

My point, however, is that Buber's writing in the quotation is hollow on its own grounds. It is false to state that by ignoring the I–Thou and genuine dialogue the description of the "They" presented by Heidegger "in itself becomes wrong." Such a statement reveals that Buber did not comprehend or evaluate in any depth the many simple and complex truths about human existence that emerge from Heideger's vivid description of the "They." Moreover, these truths—such as the ontological prevalence and the destructive power of idle talk, curiosity, and ambiguity in human relations—do not become wrong because Heidegger ignored genuine dialogue.

Buber seems to have criticized Heidegger, and other thinkers such as Kierkegaard and Sartre, with what may be termed a one-track critique. The one-track critique that Buber embraced was based on an examination of the relation of a person's thinking to the I–Thou encounter and to genuine dialogue. Such a one-track approach often ignores the valuable ideas and the provoking and profound insights that these thinkers have disclosed to their readers. The approach also gravely impoverishes Buber's own thinking and frequently makes it hollow.

* * *

I can summarize Buber's problematic discussion of *Being and Time* by noting that he correctly criticized this text for almost totally ignoring the richness and the significance of the realm of the interhuman. Buber is also right that Heidegger's presentation of human existence, and specifically his discussion of Dasein as Being-in-the-world, are skewed toward a monological existence. Buber is also correct in indicating that Heidegger's ignoring of the ontological findings presented in *I and Thou*, which was published four years before *Being and Time*, impoverish his ontology and reveal grave limits in his understanding of the human entity. An acute and correct example of Heidegger's myopia concerning human existence, mentioned by Buber, is his ignoring Dasein's relations with other persons and Dasein's activities in society in his discussion of Dasein's Being-guilty.

But it is ironic to discover that in an essay called "What Is Man?" Buber refused to see that these important and valid criticisms are not enough to dismiss all Heidegger's thinking as having little to contribute to our understanding of the whole person and of human existence. Consequently, Buber's presentation of certain ideas from *Being and Time* and his one-track critique of these ideas is quite often wrong. I find it sad, but true, to state that Buber comprehended and accepted very few of Heidegger's valuable insights and thoughtful ideas in his seminal *Being and Time*. Some of these valuable insights have been presented briefly in the first three chapters of this book.

Indeed, if you carefully review the entire Buber corpus, you will soon discover that he learned very little—if anything—from the many illuminating ideas that appear in Heidegger's fundamental ontology and also in his other writings that discuss the Being of the human entity in the world. Thus, the essay "What Is Man?"—in which much of Buber's discussion of *Being and Time* is shallow and frequently mistaken—points to a sad trend in Buber's reading of Heidegger. My research has found that this trend of superficial and unthoughtful reading of Heidegger continued throughout Buber's life. The result is unfortunate. Buber's superficial reading has rendered his own thinking quite marginal in relation to central problems that Heidegger formulated, such as the problem of truth. It is sad to conclude that this trend of superficiality opened with Buber's shallow reading of Heidegger's *Being and Time* and with his one-track critique of this major philosophical work.

I can only close this chapter, and with it Part II of this book, with a haunting question. Why did Buber blatantly ignore and disregard many of the enlightening ideas concerning the question "what is man?" that appear in Heidegger's inspiring and seminal writings, and especially in *Being and Time*?

NOTES

1. Martin Buber, "What Is Man?" in *Between Man and Man*, trans. Ronald Gregor Smith (Boston: Beacon Press, 1955), pp. 118–205.
2. Ibid., pp. 163–81.
3. Ibid., p. 163.
4. Ibid., p. 174.

Chapter 12

Conclusion and Some Implications

In the Introduction, I posed three questions which led to undertaking the research whose outcome is described in this book: What is the ontological status of the I–Thou? Do Heidegger's many enlightening insights that emerge in his fundamental ontology, insights that contributed much to twentieth-century philosophy, cast doubts upon the I–Thou that Buber articulately described? Is Buber's criticism of Heidegger's fundamental ontology, in which he argues that it ignores a major dimension of human existence that includes the I–Thou, valid? As I promised in the Introduction, these major questions have been carefully addressed in the chapters of this book.

The three questions have been explicitly answered. I have shown that Heidegger's many important insights that emerge in his fundamental ontology do not succeed in casting doubts upon the status of the I–Thou. The ontological status of the I–Thou is valid. Genuine dialogue between persons also exists. What is more, by his casting doubts on the I–Thou, I have shown that Heidegger ignored a major dimension of human existence. This dimension includes genuine dialogue, love, friendship, the I–Thou encounter, and many other personal relations that are found in the realm that Buber called the interhuman. I have also described how, by ignoring this interhuman dimension, Heidegger impoverished his fundamental ontology and his understanding of human existence. Hence, Buber's criticism of Heidegger's fundamental ontology, concerning its blatant ignoring of the I–Thou, of genuine dialogue, and of the dialogical dimension of human existence, is valid. However, I have also shown that Buber's additional criticisms of Heidegger's fundamental ontology are, unfortunately, quite mistaken.

Looking back at what has been written in this book, I perceive that something beyond fulfilling the scholarly challenge of answering the above three questions has occurred. What has happened is slightly analogous to a story that is related in chapter 9 of First Samuel in the Bible. There, we are told that Saul, the son of Kish, embarked on a search for his father's lost she-asses. Saul traveled with a boy-servant a few days on his search; but the she-asses returned home without him. Saul returned later, charged with a not yet established kingdom.

Previous chapters have shown briefly some of the profound truths and illuminating insights concerning human existence formulated by both Buber and Heidegger. Skip, for a moment, the crucial areas in which they disagree. Instead, consider those realms in which both these thinkers have illuminated and articulated the being of persons in the world and shared their wisdom with us concerning the Being of beings. We may then suddenly discover that, like Saul, each of us has been charged with a not yet established kingdom.

What is our charge? In a rather roundabout manner, this book suggests that as persons, as Beings-in-the-world, each of us can strive to be, to borrow a phrase from Heidegger, "a shepherd of Being."[1] Put succinctly, persons can endeavor to live resolutely, as Heidegger suggested, and to relate dialogically to Others, in the spirit of Buber's writings. If many persons undertake such a difficult daily challenge, we may better the human kingdom with which we all have been charged. We may even somewhat enhance the relation of human beings to the Being of beings.

* * *

But, to continue with another biblical analogue, there is no Garden of Eden without the serpent. In the chapters above, I have here and there hinted at the existence of the specific serpent that raises its head in the writings of both Heidegger and Buber, proffering an apple from the tree of knowledge of Good and Evil. In the context of this book, I would name this serpent political freedom. This serpent advises us to not be satisfied with living resolutely and dialogically. We must also, through action, assume responsibility for justice and for the fate of the world. I would also hold that neither Buber nor Heidegger has dared to taste the apple that this serpent proffers.

To be more specific, let us assume that we can unite the enlightening insights articulated and described in the fundamental ontology of Heidegger with the dialogical possibilities of human existence, including the speaking of the primary word *Thou*, that Buber described. We would soon discover that, in this integrated ontology, knowledge both of Good and Evil and of justice and injustice in the world is sorely lacking. Also lacking is an understanding of each person's responsibility in the world, on the basis of this knowledge of Good and Evil and of justice and injustice. For instance, Heidegger never suggests an even partial answer, linked to everyday life, to the rather simple question, What are my specific personal responsibilities as a shepherd of Being?

Buber explains that responsibility comes into being when a person responds wholeheartedly to the appeal of a partner in dialogue. I agree. But such a response is a very limited, albeit important, realm of personal responsibility. It excludes many other major responsibilities that are included in my responsibility for the fate of the world.

To give just one example, Buber's realm of responsibility does not include my personal responsibility for the terrible degrading poverty of one billion two hundred million people, who are my fellow sojourners on the face of the earth. Much of the abysmal poverty that these hundreds of millions of men, women, and children suffer daily is a result of wicked economic policies and pernicious political decisions promoted by business and political leaders in the wealthy nations of the world. It is to these wealthy nations that I belong. Nothing in Buber's description of personal responsibility, as linked to dialogue, can suggest how I should act so as to bring justice to these hundreds of millions of unjustly impoverished people of the world.

Much the same criticism, if not harsher, can be leveled against Heidegger's ontology, including his concept of care. I will not describe this criticism in detail. I have briefly hinted, in previous chapters, that Heidegger's enlightening ontology does not show us that Dasein also may exist on the political level, where a person is responsible for justice and injustice. Nor does his fundamental ontology have any immediate implications that might help a person distinguish between Good and Evil. Might his relentless ignoring of the political dimension of human existence be a reason that Heidegger succumbed so easily, in the 1930s, to the lure of Nazism? Might this blatant ignoring of political existence, and with it political responsibility, also be the reason that he never repented his adherence to Nazism?

Consequently, if we wish to taste of the apple of knowledge of Good and Evil, proffered by the serpent called political freedom, it will bring many changes in our evaluation of and adherence to Heidegger's and Buber's brilliant thinking. Put differently, we must know that if we decide to cope with the problem of justice, either on the philosophical level or on the practical level, our decision will bring us to a situation wherein we will have to abandon the ontological Garden of Eden established by the joint wisdom of Buber and Heidegger. We will then find ourselves cast out of this insightful ontological garden and forced to deal, on our own, with the problems of Good and Evil. We will also have to relate, both on the ontological and the practical level, to the justice and injustice that exists in the world.

After tasting the apple and being evicted from Eden, we will find that living wholly, and with responsibility for the fate of the world, requires that we respond to the challenge of pursuing justice. Need I add that undertaking such a challenge—on both the ontological and the practical level—adds much integrity to a person's Being-in-the-world?

This exile from the ontology of Heidegger and Buber into a world where you are challenged to pursue justice, may lead to many new and exciting findings. But even partially describing such a new ontological path of existence deserves a new study. At this point, I can only suggest that for such a philosophical study to be valid and worthy, we dare not ignore the profound ontological insights that we have been fortunate to receive from Martin Heidegger and Martin Buber.

NOTE

1. Martin Heidegger, "Letter on Humanism," in *Basic Writings*, ed. David Farrell Krell (New York: Harper & Row, 1977), p. 210.

Selected Bibliography

Arendt, Hannah. *The Human Condition*. Chicago: University of Chicago Press, 1958.

Bernasconi, Robert. *Heidegger in Question*. Atlantic Highlands, N.J.: Humanities Press, 1993.

Buber, Martin. *Between Man and Man*, trans. Ronald Gregor Smith. Boston: Beacon Press, 1955.

———. *Eclipse of God*. New York: Harper & Row, 1952.

———. *Good and Evil*. New York: Scribner's, 1952.

———. *I and Thou*, trans. Ronald Gregor Smith. New York: Scribner's, 1958.

———. *Kingship of God*, trans. Richard Scheimann. Atlantic Highlands, N.J.: Humanities Press, 1967.

———. *The Knowledge of Man*, trans. Maurice Friedman and Ronald Gregor Smith. New York: Harper & Row, 1965.

———. *Pointing the Way*, trans. Maurice Friedman. New York: Harper & Row, 1957.

———. *Tales of the Hasidim: Early Masters*, trans. Olga Marx. New York: Schocken Books, 1947.

———. *Tales of the Hasidim: Later Masters*, trans. Olga Marx. New York: Schocken Books, 1948.

Chomsky, Noam. *Deterring Democracy*. London: Verso, 1991.

Dallmayr, Fred. *The Other Heidegger*. Ithaca, N.Y.: Cornell University Press, 1993.

Dostoyevsky, Fyodor. *The Brothers Karamazov*, trans. Richard Pevear and Larissa Volokhonsky. New York: Vintage, 1991.

Dreyfus, Hubert L. *Being-in-the-World*. Cambridge, Mass.: MIT Press, 1991.

———, and Harrison Hall, eds. *Heidegger: A Critical Reader*. Oxford, Eng.: Basil Blackwell, 1992.

Gadamer, Hans-George. *Heidegger's Ways*, trans. John W. Stanley. Albany, N.Y.: State University of New York Press, 1994.

Gordon, Haim. *Dance, Dialogue, and Despair: Existentialist Philosophy and Education for Peace in Israel*. Tuscaloosa: University of Alabama Press, 1986.

———. *Dwelling Poetically: Educational Challenges in Heidegger's Thinking on Poetry*. Amsterdam: Rodopi, 2000.

———. *Fighting Evil: Unsung Heroes in the Novels of Graham Greene*. Westport, Conn.: Greenwood Press, 1997.

———. *Quicksand: Israel, the Intifada, and the Rise of Political Evil in Democracies*. East Lansing: Michigan State University Press, 1995.

———, and Jochanan Bloch. *Martin Buber: A Centenary Volume*. New York: Ktav, 1984.

———, and Rivca Gordon. *Sartre and Evil: Guidelines for a Struggle*. Westport, Conn.: Greenwood Press, 1995.

Guignon, Charles, ed. *The Cambridge Companion to Heidegger*. Cambridge, Eng.: Cambridge University Press, 1993.

Haar, Michel. *Heidegger and the Essence of Man*, trans. William McNeill. Albany: State University of New York Press, 1993.

Heidegger, Martin. *Basic Concepts*, trans. Gary E. Aylesworth. Bloomington: Indiana University Press, 1993.

———. *The Basic Problems of Phenomenology*, trans. Albert Hofstadter. Bloomington: Indiana University Press, 1982.

———. *Basic Writings*, ed. David Farrell Krell. New York: Harper & Row, 1977.

———. *Being and Time*, trans. John Macquarrie and Edward Robinson. Oxford, Eng.: Basil Blackwell, 1962.

———. *Holderlin's Hymn "The Ister,"* trans. William McNeill and Julia Davis. Bloomington: Indiana University Press, 1996.

———. *Kant and the Problem of Metaphysics*, trans. Richard Taft. Bloomington: Indiana University Press, 1990.

———. *The Metaphysical Foundations of Logic*, trans. Michael Heim. Bloomington: Indiana University Press, 1984.

———. *On the Way to Language*, trans. Peter D. Hertz. New York: Harper & Row, 1982.

———. *Parmenides*, trans. Andre Schuwer and Richard Rojcewicz. Bloomington: Indiana University Press, 1992.

———. *Pathmarks*, ed. William McNeill. Cambridge, Eng.: Cambridge University Press, 1998.

———. *Phenomenological Interpretation of Kant's "Critique of Pure Reason,"* trans. Parvis Emad and Kenneth Maly. Bloomington: Indiana University Press, 1997.

———. *Poetry, Language, Thought*, trans. Albert Hofstadter. New York: Harper & Row, 1971.

Kierkegaard, Søren. *The Concept of Anxiety*, trans. Reidar Thomte with Albert B. Anderson. Princeton, N.J.: Princeton University Press, 1980.

———. *Either/Or*, vol. 1, trans. David F. Swenson and Lillian Marvin Swenson. Princeton, N.J.: Princeton University Press, 1959.

Kockelmans, Joseph J., ed. *On Heidegger and Language*. Evanston, Ill.: Northwestern University Press, 1972.

Macann, Christopher, ed. *Critical Heidegger*. London: Routledge, 1996.

Neruda, Pablo. *The Captain's Verses*, trans. Donald D. Walsh. New York: New Directions, 1972.

———. *100 Love Sonnets*, trans. Stephen Tapscott. Austin: Texas University Press, 1986.

Plato. *The Collected Dialogues*, ed. Edith Hamilton and Huntington Cairns. Princeton, N.J.: Princeton University Press, 1961.

Poe, Edgar Allan. *Poems and Essays on Poetry*, ed. C. H. Sisson. Manchester, Eng.: Carcanet, 1995.

Poggeler, Otto. *Martin Heidegger's Path of Thinking*, trans. Daniel Magurshak and Sigmund Barber. Atlantic Highlands, N.J.: Humanities Press, 1987.

Polt, Richard. *Heidegger: An Introduction*. London: UCL Press, 1999.

Proust, Marcel. *Remembrance of Things Past*, trans. C. K. Scott Moncrieff. New York: Random House, 1934.

Sallis, John, ed. *Reading Heidegger: Commemorations*. Bloomington: Indiana University Press, 1993.

Sartre, Jean-Paul. *Existentialism and Humanism*, trans. Philip Mairet. London: Methuen, 1948.

———. *Nausea*, trans. Robert Baldick. London: Penguin, 1963.

Schlipp, Paul Arthur, and Maurice Friedman. *The Philosophy of Martin Buber*. La Salle, Ill.: Open Court. 1967.

Shakespeare, William. *The Complete Works of William Shakespeare*. Cleveland, Ohio: World Syndicate.

Tolstoy, Leo. *Anna Karenina*, trans. David Magarshack. New York: New American Library, 1961.

Wolin, Richard. *The Heidegger Controversy*. Cambridge, Mass.: MIT Press, 1993.

Wood, Robert E. *Martin Buber's Ontology: An Analysis of "I and Thou."* Evanston, Ill.: Northwestern University Press, 1969.

Index

Adler, Alfred, 70
Anaximander, xvi
Anxiety, 33–34, 42, 44–45, 51
Aquinas, Saint Thomas. *See* Thomas
  Aquinas, Saint
Aristotle, xvi, 73, 77
Athens, 146
Auschwitz, 144

Balzac, Honoré de, 82
Beauvoir, Simone de, xv
Beethoven, Ludwig van, 79
Being, ix, xiv, xvi–xvii, 5–8, 10–11, 14–
  15, 19, 23–24, 26, 28–31, 33–37, 44,
  49, 51–54, 63–65, 67–68, 73–75, 77,
  80, 83–84, 87, 92, 102, 104, 108, 116,
  147, 152–153, 155, 160
Being-free, 34–35, 37
Being-guilty, 48–52, 154
Being-in, 8–11, 23, 27, 29, 33
Being-in-the-world, 5–17, 23–24, 27,
  29, 33–36, 38, 41–42, 45, 48, 50, 53–
  54, 56, 58, 71–72, 78–79, 81, 85, 87,
  93–96, 100, 103, 105–107, 116, 119,
  121, 133–134, 148, 154, 157, 160, 162
Being-there, 23–24, 47

Being-toward-death, xiv, 41–43, 44, 52
Being-with, 6, 15, 18–19, 20, 27–28, 31,
  48, 57–58, 66, 79, 95, 103, 106–107,
  121–122, 154
Berdyaev, Nikolai, 94
The Between, 14, 59, 115
Bible, xi, xvi–xvii, 139, 145, 160
Block, Jochanan, xiv–xv
British colonialist regime, 126
Buber, Martin, ix–xviii, 6–7, 11, 14, 21,
  29, 48, 59, 83, 85, 86–88, 93–95, 102,
  108, 115–123, 125–134, 139–149, 151–
  157, 159–162. *Works: Between Man
  and Man*, x; "Dialogue," 140–143,
  149; "Distance and Relation," 148;
  Eclipse of God, x; "Elements of the
  Interhuman," 134, 146–147, 149;
  Hasidic tales, xv; *I and Thou*, xi–xiii,
  xvi–xvii, 86, 94–95, 115–117, 122–
  123, 125–126, 131–132, 134, 139–141,
  143, 146–149, 157; *Ich und Du*, ix;
  "The Question to the Single One,"
  143–144, 146, 149; "What Is Man?,"
  x, 48, 140, 148, 151–153, 157

California, 37
Camus, Albert, xv

Care, 33–35, 41, 55
Cassirer, Ernst, 92
Cicero, 7, 93; *On Friendship*, 7
Collectivism, 146
Conrad, Joseph, 106–107, 116
Copernican revolution, 27, 115–116
Copernicus, Nicolaus, 9, 27

Dasein, xi, xiv, xvii, 5–21, 23–38, 41–45, 47–59, 64–75, 77–88, 95–96, 101–108, 116, 119, 121, 132–134, 148, 152–155, 157
Decalogue, 145
Descartes, René, 11, 66–68, 70, 141
Dostoyevsky, Fyodor, 17–18, 25, 52, 107; *The Brothers Karamazov*, 17, 25, 107

Ebener, Ferdinand, xii
Egoicity, 101–102
Einstein, Albert, 13
Eternal Thou, 118

Feuerbach, Ludwig Andreas, xii, 141; *Principles of the Philosophy of the Future*, xii
First Samuel, 160
Franco, Francisco, 16
Freedom, 17, 18, 45, 49, 101, 146, 160
Freud, Sigmund, 66, 70
Frost, Robert, 81

Galileo (Galileo Galilei), 27
Gandhi, Mohandas Karamchand "Mahatma," 44, 126, 146
Garden of Eden, 160–161
Germany, 63, 68, 91, 143
Greece, 145
Greek philosophy, xvi, 108

Hasidim, xvi, 139
Hebrew prophets, xi
Hebrew University, x, 151
Heidegger, Martin, ix–xviii, 5–21, 23, 24–38, 41–42, 44–45, 48–59, 63–75, 77–78, 91–97, 99–108, 116, 119, 121–123, 132–134, 140–141, 144–145, 148,

151–157, 159–163. *Works: The Basic Problems of Phenomenology*, ix, 63–64, 67–68, 73, 77, 88; *Being and Time*, ix–x, xiii–xv, xvii, 5–6, 14, 18, 26, 29, 35, 41, 58–59, 63–64, 69, 71, 73, 77, 80, 83–85, 92–94, 99, 116, 134, 151–157; *Kant and the Problem of Metaphysics*, 91–92; "Letter on Humanism," xi; *The Metaphysical Foundations of Logic*, x, 99–100, 107; Phenomenological Interpretation of Kant's "Critique of Pure Reason," ix, 91, 93, 97; "The Question Concerning Technology," 29; *Sein und Zeit*, ix
Heisenberg, Werner, 14
Hemingway, Ernest, xiii
Heraclitus, xvi
Hesiod, 37, 145
Hitler, Adolf, 16
Hobbes, Thomas, 73
Hölderlin, Friedrich, x, 6
Horwitz, Rivka, xii
Human rights, 23, 144
Humanism, 5
Humboldt, Baron Wilhelm von, 141
Husserl, Edmund, xvi

Idle talk, 28–32, 73
I–It, ix, xvi, 86, 117–118, 122, 125–126, 128, 133–134, 145–146
India, 126
Individualism, 146
Intentionality, 64–66, 70–71
Israelis, 144
I–Thou, ix–xviii, 6, 14, 18, 29, 38, 58–59, 63–64, 66, 75, 77, 81, 83–88, 91, 94–97, 100, 101–103, 105, 107–108, 115–123, 125–126, 132–134, 139–143, 145–148, 153, 156, 159

Jerusalem, 151
Jesus, 140
Jung, Carl Gustav, 66, 70
Justice, 7, 19, 35, 88, 144–146, 160–161

Kafka, Franz, 129
Kant, Immanuel, xvi, 13, 53, 64, 66–
    70, 91–93, 95, 115–116, 151; *Critique
    of Pure Reason*, 91–93
Kierkegaard, Søren Aabye, xv, 24, 34,
    93, 127–131, 143–144, 149, 156; *Ei-
    ther/Or*, 127
Kissinger, Henry, 69
Knowledge, 8–9, 24, 27, 30–32, 84

Leibnitz, Baron Gottfried Wilhelm
    von, xvi, 6, 103
Lotze, Rudolf Hermann, 73

Mahler, Gustav, 6
Mandela, Nelson, 44, 126, 146
Marcel, Gabriel, xii, xv, 94
Merleau-Ponty, Maurice, 70, 148
Michelangelo, Buonarroti, 80
Mill, John Stewart, 73
Moser, Simon, 63
Moses, 145
Moslems, 9
Mount Sinai, 145
Mozart, Wolfgang Amadeus, 70, 118
Mussolini, Benito, 16

Nature, 10
Nazi Germany, 151
Nazis, xii
Nazism, xvii, 161
Neruda, Pablo, 52, 69, 120–121
Newton, Sir Isaac, 13, 37
Nietzsche, Friedrich Wilhelm, xvi

Orthodox Jews, 9
Ott, Heinrich, xi; "Hermeneutic and
    Personal Structure of Language," xi

Palestine, 151
Palestinians, 23, 144
Parmenides, xvi
Pinochet, Augusto, 16
Plato, xvi, 7, 18, 28, 30, 35, 49, 52, 93,
    108, 128, 141–142, 145. *Works: Phae-
    drus*, 7, 28, 108; *The Republic*, 35, 145;
    The Symposium, 108; *Theatetus*, 30

Poe, Edgar Allan, 52, 119–120, 128;
    "Annabel Lee," 52, 119–121
Poggeler, Otto, x, 5; *Martin Heidegger's
    Path of Thinking*, x
Political realm, 144–146
Pre-Socratic Philosophers, xvi
Proust, Marcel, xv, 15, 54; *Remem-
    brance of Things Past*, 15, 54

Ramadan, 9
Resoluteness, 50–53, 84–85
Resolution, 56–57
Rilke, Rainer Maria, 71; *The Notebooks
    of Malte Laurids Brigge*, 71–72
Rosenzweig, Franz, 134
Russell, Bertrand, 106–107, 116; *Por-
    traits from Memory and Other Essays*,
    106

Saadia Gaon, 9
Sartre, Jean-Paul, xv, 7, 20, 68, 70, 144,
    148, 156; *Nausea*, 21
Saul (son of Kish), 160
Scheler, Max, xvi
Schelling, Friedrich Wilhelm Joseph
    von, xvi
Schönberg, Arnold, 13; *Moses and
    Aaron*, 13
Scotus, Duns, 67
Shakespeare, William, xv, 31, 47, 49,
    51–52, 100, 104–106, 119, 121, 128,
    153. *Works: Hamlet*, 153; *Julius Cae-
    sar*, 31; *Romeo and Juliet*, 100, 106,
    119, 121
Socrates, 18, 28, 30, 44, 142, 146
Song of Songs, 120
South Africa, 126, 144
Stalin, Joseph, 16
Suárez, Francisco, 67

Technology, 5
Temporality, 54–59, 79, 80–81, 85
The "They," 19–21, 28–29, 31–34, 37,
    43–45, 47–51, 53–54, 56, 73, 84, 88,
    133, 156
Thomas Aquinas, Saint, 67, 141
Time, 55, 59, 78–81, 116

Tolstoy, Leo, xiii, xv, 32, 52, 130; *Anna Karenina*, 32, 130–131
Truth, 10, 33, 36–38, 44, 45, 50, 73–74

University of Freiburg, x, 99
University of Marburg, ix–x, 63, 88, 91, 99
Urrutia, Matilde, 69, 120

Vermeer, Jan, 118
Vogel, Lawrence P., xi; *The Fragile*

"We": *Ethical Implications of Heidegger's "Being and Time,"* xi

Western philosophers, xvi
Wonder, 30
Wood, Robert E., xi; *Martin Buber's Ontology: An Analysis of "I and Thou,"* xi

Yom Kippur, 9

About the Author

HAIM GORDON is full professor in the Department of Education at Ben Gurion University of the Negev. He has published widely in the fields of philosophy and education. Among his recent books are *Dictionary of Existentialism* (1999), *Looking Back at the June 1967 War* (1999), and *Fighting Evil: Unsung Heroes in the Novels of Graham Greene* (1997).